MICHAEL SYMON'S

5 IN 5

5 FRESH INGREDIENTS
+ 5 MINUTES
= 120 FANTASTIC DINNERS

MICHAEL SYMON'S

IN

MICHAEL SYMON
WITH DOUGLAS TRATTNER

PHOTOGRAPHS
BY JENNIFER MAY

 Clarkson Potter/
Publishers
New York

Copyright © 2013 by Michael Symon
Photographs copyright © 2013 by Jennifer May

Published in the United States by Clarkson Potter/Publishers, an imprint of the
Crown Publishing Group, a division of Random House, Inc., New York.
www.crownpublishing.com
www.clarksonpotter.com

CLARKSON POTTER is a trademark and POTTER with colophon is a registered
trademark of Random House, Inc.

Library of Congress Cataloging-in-Publication Data
Symon, Michael
  Michael Symon's 5 in 5 / Michael Symon with Douglas Trattner.
     pages cm
  Includes index.
1. Quick and easy cooking. 2. Cooking, American. I. Trattner, Douglas II. Title. III.
Title: 5 in 5. IV. Title: Michael Symon's five in five.

 TX833.5.S98 2013
 641.5'55--dc23

                                    2013004299
ISBN 978-0-7704-3432-8
eISBN 978-0-7704-3433-5

Printed in the United States of America

Book and cover design by Laura Palese
Cover photographs by Jennifer May

10 9 8 7 6 5 4 3 2

First Edition

TO LIZ, KYLE, AND THE REST
OF MY WONDERFUL FAMILY,
who have instilled in me not only
an appreciation of good food, but
also the awareness of how good
food can bring a family together.

CONTENTS

INTRODUCTION

When I was first asked to join ABC's
***The Chew,* what excited me most**
was the thought of being able to
inspire people at home to cook simple,
affordable, and delicious food.

Up to that point in my career, most of the cooking I had been doing—both at my restaurants and on television—was high-end restaurant-style food. I absolutely love competing on *Iron Chef America,* but let's face it: Not a lot of viewers are going to have the time, ingredients, or skill to make those dishes at home for dinner.

So while we were devising different segments for the show, I thought it would be great to do something that was practical and encouraging. My goal was to show people that cooking doesn't have to be intimidating or time-consuming or expensive to be delicious. If I motivated even a few viewers to cook more often at home, then I would consider my mission a success.

I didn't have to look too far for inspiration. The truth of the matter is that Liz and I don't go out to dinner very often. And after a long day in the studio or my restaurants, I don't always feel like whipping up an elaborate feast, either. More often than not, I look in the fridge, look in the pantry, and come up with a quick meal based on what we already have on hand. Not only does this cooking style eliminate the need to run to the store, it is also extremely cost-effective, another plus.

Knowing that home cooks, like me, don't always want to spend hours in the kitchen making a meal, I decided that the recipes should be quick, too. How quick? Well, what if I could trim that time to as little as 5 minutes. I thought, *Who wouldn't cook more if they knew they could prepare a great meal in less than the time it takes to listen to "Stairway to Heaven"?*

Thus, *5 in 5* was born. Using no more than 5 fresh ingredients and some pantry staples, which all cook in 5 minutes, you can make dinner for a family of four every night and—bonus—that meal will cost less than $5 a serving. To make it fun on the show, we decided to do a beat-the-clock-style bit, not unlike what I've been doing for years on *Iron Chef America*. It's become one of the most popular segments on *The Chew*.

Now keep in mind that I've been cooking professionally for decades and can work pretty quickly. But on the show, even I sometimes go over the buzzer—and it's always a riot! The key is to relax, have fun, and cook more. If it takes you 6, 7, or even—gasp!—8 minutes, so be it. In the end, you will still end up with a delicious, made-from-scratch meal that costs less than fast food, tastes a million times better, and is healthier for you and your family.

THE 5 IN 5 PANTRY

It's no secret that a well-stocked pantry is the key to cooking quick, affordable, and delicious meals. The kitchen cupboard is the foundation upon which all meals are built, and having a broad and deep bench means never having to run out in the rain to make dinner.

Because pantry items are nonperishable, they can last for months and months. That's why I like to err on the side of acquisition over scarcity. I just love going into a great specialty store and experimenting with a new vinegar, whole-grain mustard, or exotic spice blend.

That's not to say you need a ton of obscure ingredients to make the recipes in this book. In fact, I stuck to basics, which I outline here, in these recipes. And I'm not going to give you an exhaustive list of every single item you *should* have in your pantry—just a simple list as to what you'll want to have on hand to make many of the recipes in this book.

Beyond the basic staples like sugar, flour, cornstarch, **kosher salt,** and **whole black peppercorns** (you *do* grind your pepper fresh, right?), there are certain items I always have on hand. You need some kind of oil in most recipes, and you can go crazy with all the different types that are available at stores. I tend to use the more affordable regular **olive oil** for cooking and pan-frying, and a good-quality **extra-virgin olive oil** for vinaigrettes and for drizzling.

When it comes to pasta, the dried variety can't be beat for ease of use and shelf life. I always keep boxes and boxes of **different varieties of dried pasta** around because some noodles work better with some sauces than others. That said, good **fresh pasta** wins when it comes to texture and speed of cooking time. But fresh pasta won't last forever, even in the fridge. **Couscous,** a quick-cooking pasta, is another brilliant dried staple to have on hand.

I have towers of canned San Marzano tomatoes—whole, diced, and crushed—because they are always ripe and "in season." Open up a can in January and they will taste exactly like the ones you opened in August: sweet, juicy, and delicious. And when it comes to cooking, consistency is the goal. Of course, I also use fresh tomatoes for certain recipes, especially in summer, but canned Italian tomatoes are perfect for most uses. Along these same lines: I have no problem using good-quality canned broths and canned beans at home, even if I never use them at my restaurants.

One of the secrets to great cooking is knowing when and how to introduce acid to your dishes. Acid, in the form of vinegar or fresh citrus, accentuates all the other flavors in the dish. I am a vinegar fanatic, and I generally have a shelf-ful of tasty varieties. For our purposes, you need only to stock white wine, red wine, sherry, balsamic, and cider vinegars to cook every recipe in this book. Vinegar has an indefinite shelf life, so there's no reason not to grab a few different bottles.

My other can't-live-without bottled pantry items include capers, soy sauce, hot sauce, Dijon mustard, Marsala wine, and honey. When it comes to spices needed to whip up every recipe in this book, you'll need coriander, cinnamon, cumin, caraway, cayenne, celery seed, chipotle powder, ancho chile powder, smoked paprika, crushed red pepper flakes, and sesame seeds.

I usually tend to have some bread on hand, whether for breakfast or for making sandwiches. Well-wrapped, a loaf can last on the counter for a few days and in the fridge or freezer even longer. I slice leftovers and bring them back to life in the toaster. For breading, you'll need plain dry bread crumbs or, my personal favorite, panko bread crumbs.

When it comes to the 5 or fewer fresh ingredients that go into each recipe, the good news is that you will likely already have many of those on hand, too, though I bolded those in each recipe so you can do a quick check. Fridge staples like butter, eggs, cheese, and mayo are considered fresh for purposes of this book, as are cellar veggies like garlic and onions. If you keep a garden, you may also grow a number of the fresh herbs, including basil, dill, cilantro, mint, and parsley. And if you are anything like me, you'll have no shortage of ripe tomatoes come late summer.

That leaves just the meat, fish, fruit, and a few veggies that you'll have to pick up on your way home. Oh, and the bacon. Whatever you do, do not forget the bacon!

5 IN 5 QUICK BUILDS

There are a ton of great recipes in here, and you can eat well for weeks on end cooking them just as they are written. But I hope this cookbook will also help you build confidence, experiment, and become fearless in the kitchen.

If you look at these recipes not as commands but rather as suggestions, I think the possibilities become almost endless. Breaking up each recipe into its building blocks, for many of them you end up with a protein, a few fresh ingredients, and a few pantry ingredients. I encourage you—challenge, really—to mix and match the components of one recipe with another, and vice versa. I promise you that while some combinations might work better than others, almost none will flop either. And, who knows, maybe you'll come up with a recipe or three that are better than anything in here!

What follows is a chart of some of my personal favorite flavor pairings. Use it as a guide to customize the recipes in this book—or to create your very own. Just be sure to think about balancing fat and salt with freshness and acidity—and crunch!

MY FAVORITE FLAVORS WITH
PORK

FRESH HERBS & AROMATICS	FRUITS & VEGGIES	DAIRY	PANTRY
Cilantro	Lime	Parmesan	Cider vinegar
Flat-leaf parsley	Apples	Manchego	Sherry vinegar
Mint	Broccoli rabe	Feta	Soy sauce
Sage	Peaches	Butter	Dijon mustard
Garlic	Figs		Honey
Ginger	Scallions		Peanuts
	Arugula		Slivered almonds
	Broccoli		
	Peas		

SEE

Angel Hair with Peas & Pancetta (page 31)	Pork Cutlet with Peaches & Almonds (page 163)	Pork Tenderloin with Soy, Ginger & Cilantro (page 63)	Breaded Pork Loin with Apple Salad (page 136)
=	=	=	=
mint	flat-leaf parsley	garlic	flat-leaf parsley
+ garlic	+ peaches	+ ginger	+ apple
+ peas	+ butter	+ cilantro	+ scallions
+ Parmesan	+ sherry vinegar	+ lime	+ cider vinegar
	+ slivered almonds	+ soy sauce	+ Dijon mustard
		+ honey	+ honey

MY FAVORITE FLAVORS WITH
BEEF

FRESH HERBS & AROMATICS	FRUITS & VEGGIES	DAIRY	PANTRY
Flat-leaf parsley	Lime	Parmesan	Dry red wine
Oregano	Lemon	Blue cheese	Balsamic vinegar
Cilantro	Arugula	Swiss cheese	Sherry vinegar
Rosemary	Baby spinach	Greek yogurt	Worcestershire sauce
Basil	Corn		Black pepper
Garlic	Mushrooms		Red pepper flakes
	Red onion		Coriander
	Scallions		San Marzano tomatoes
			Chickpeas
			Peanuts
			Hazelnuts

SEE

Grilled Skirt Steak with Chickpea Salad (page 200)	Grilled Flank Steak with Corn & Bacon Salad (page 196)	Beef Satay with Cilantro Pesto (page 65)	Breaded Beef Cutlet with Spinach & Mushroom Salad (page 148)
=	=	=	=
flat-leaf parsley	corn	cilantro	red onion
+ scallions	+ arugula	+ Parmesan	+ button mushrooms
+ Greek yogurt	+ red onion	+ coriander	+ baby spinach
+ coriander	+ sherry vinegar	+ red pepper flakes	+ balsamic vinegar
+ chickpeas		+ hazelnuts	

MY FAVORITE FLAVORS WITH
POULTRY

FRESH HERBS & AROMATICS	FRUITS & VEGGIES	DAIRY	PANTRY
Flat-leaf parsley	Frisée	Butter	Dry white wine
Sage	Lemon	Greek yogurt	Red wine vinegar
Tarragon	Orange	Fresh mozzarella	Cider vinegar
Rosemary	Arugula	Parmesan cheese	Soy sauce
Cilantro	Asparagus		Capers
Garlic			Kalamata olives
			Dijon mustard
			San Marzano tomatoes
			Sliced almonds
			Smoked paprika

SEE

Turkey Cutlet with Lemon, Capers & Brown Butter (page 164)	Chicken with Brown Butter & Orange (page 179)	Chicken Paillard Salad (page 135)	Chicken with Spicy Yogurt & Cilantro (page 71)
=	=	=	=
sage	flat-leaf parsley	tarragon	cilantro
+ lemon	+ orange	+ frisée	+ orange
+ butter	+ butter	+ Dijon mustard	+ Greek yogurt
+ capers	+ sliced almonds	+ red wine vinegar	+ smoked paprika

MY FAVORITE FLAVORS WITH
FISH &
SEAFOOD

FRESH HERBS & AROMATICS	FRUITS & VEGGIES	DAIRY	PANTRY
Mint	Lemon	Feta	Dry white wine
Flat-leaf parsley	Lime	Sour cream	White wine vinegar
Cilantro	Orange	Greek yogurt	Sherry vinegar
Dill	Grapefuit	Butter	Capers
Ginger	Pineapple		Dijon mustard
	Carrots		Red pepper flakes
	Green beans		Cumin
	Baby spinach		Chipotle powder
	Avocado		Sliced almonds
	Cucumber		
	Red onion		

SEE

Grilled Shrimp & Grapefruit Salad (page 203)	Grilled Salmon with Shaved Cucumbers (page 207)	Grilled Salmon & Avocado Salad (page 185)	Trout & Green Beans (page 153)
=	=	=	=
flat-leaf parsley	dill	cilantro	lemon
+ grapefruit	+ cucumber	+ lime	+ green beans
+ red onion	+ sour cream	+ avocado	+ sliced almonds
+ avocado	+ white wine vinegar	+ chipotle powder	

MY FAVORITE FLAVORS WITH
PASTA

FRESH HERBS & AROMATICS	FRUITS & VEGGIES	DAIRY	PANTRY	MEAT & SEAFOOD
Basil	Peas	Parmesan	Extra-virgin olive oil	Pancetta
Chives	Tomatoes	Manchego	White wine	Chorizo
Flat-leaf parsley	Kale	Aged cheddar	Red pepper flakes	Guanciale
Mint	Lemon	Feta	San Marzano tomatoes	Bacon
Oregano	Jalapeño	Fresh mozzarella	Chickpeas	Spicy Italian sausage
Tarragon	Broccoli	Goat cheese	Pine nuts	Mussels
Garlic	Cauliflower	Sour cream		White anchovies
	Corn			Olive oil–packed tuna
	Mushrooms			
	Baby spinach			

SEE

Angel Hair with Corn, Feta & Tomato (page 39)	Rigatoni with Chorizo & Manchego (page 43)	Penne with Broccoli, Aged Cheddar & Bacon (page 52)	Spaghetti with Mussels & Tomato (page 50)	Shells with Tuna, Chickpeas & Parsley (page 58)
=	=	=	=	=
corn	chorizo	bacon	mussels	olive oil–packed tuna
+ oregano	+ San Marzano tomatoes	+ broccoli	+ jalapeño	+ chickpeas
+ tomatoes	+ white wine	+ aged cheddar	+ San Marzano tomatoes	+ lemon
+ feta	+ Manchego	+ pine nuts	+ basil	+ flat-leaf parsley

MY FAVORITE FLAVORS IN
SANDWICHES

FRESH HERBS & AROMATICS	FRUITS & VEGGIES	DAIRY	PANTRY	MEAT & SEAFOOD
Basil	Avocado	Provolone	Red wine vinegar	Italian sausage
Cilantro	Jalapeño	Parmesan	San Marzano tomatoes	Bologna
Flat-leaf parsley	Broccoli rabe	Monterey Jack	Capers	Salami
Garlic	Red bell pepper	Swiss cheese	Kalamata olives	Bacon
	Tomatoes	Gruyère	Red pepper flakes	Chorizo
	Arugula	Blue cheese	Dijon mustard	Pork loin
	Scallions	Fresh mozzarella	Hot sauce	Rib eye
	Sundried tomatoes		Mayonnaise	Ground beef
				Smoked turkey breast
				Chicken thighs
				Olive oil–packed tuna

SEE

Fried Salami with Hot Peppers (page 83)	Ultimate BLT (page 99)	Pork Cutlet with Broccoli Rabe (page 90)	Tuna Niçoise Salad Sandwich (page 102)	Turkey & Avocado Melt (page 96)
=	=	=	=	=
basil	tomato	broccoli rabe	sundried tomatoes	avocado
+ jalapeño	+ basil	+ Parmesan	+ kalamata olives	+ Gruyère
+ provolone	+ avocado	+ garlic	+ Swiss cheese	+ Dijon mustard
	+ Dijon mustard	+ red pepper flakes	+ flat-leaf parsley	+ mayonnaise
	+ hot sauce		+ red pepper flakes	

23

TIMESAVING TIPS

I know, 5 minutes does not sound like a lot of time. That's because it isn't! If you watch me on *The Chew*, you already know that I sometimes go over the 5-minute mark. And you may too—but that's okay, because the last I checked, the goal isn't to beat the clock; it's to enjoy a delicious and affordable home-cooked meal with your family.

That said, there are certain things you can do to give yourself a time advantage:

- Get that **pasta water going** the minute everyone gets home.

- **Plan ahead.** Read through the entire recipe before you start so there are no surprises.

- **Get to know your butcher** so you can purchase boned meats, pounded meats, cubed meats, shaved meats, and many other prepped ingredients that are used throughout this book.

- **Take meat and fish out of the fridge** ahead of time to give them a chance to come to room temperature.

- Have all your **herbs and veggies washed, cut, and ready** to go before you begin cooking.

- **Cut your ingredients to a consistent size** so they all finish cooking at the same time.

- **Preheat your grill, grill pan, or skillet** so it is hot and ready to go when needed.

- When you read the word **"meanwhile"** in a recipe, that means that step should be done while something else is cooking.

- If the recipe calls for **toasted bread or buns,** don't wait until the last minute to get them going.

- If you plan on making any of the "On a Stick" recipes (pages 60–73), **soak your wooden skewers in water** for at least 30 minutes to prevent flames. Salting the water will help the skewers flavor the meat from the inside, too.

- Have all your **plates or platters ready** to go so the food doesn't get cold while you're finding them.

ANGEL HAIR WITH TOMATOES & GARLIC 29

ANGEL HAIR WITH PEAS & PANCETTA 31

CAVATELLI WITH CAULIFLOWER & RED PEPPER FLAKES 32

ANGEL HAIR WITH BACON & TOMATOES 34

ORECCHIETTE WITH MUSHROOMS, SPINACH & GOAT CHEESE 35

ANGEL HAIR WITH CORN, FETA & TOMATO 39

SPAGHETTI WITH OLIVE OIL, GARLIC & RED PEPPER FLAKES 40

TAGLIATELLE WITH QUICK MEAT SAUCE 42

PASTA

RIGATONI WITH CHORIZO & MANCHEGO 43

ORECCHIETTE WITH SAUSAGE & KALE 45

NO-BAKE MAC & CHEESE 46

PAPPARDELLE WITH MUSHROOM CREAM SAUCE 49

SPAGHETTI WITH MUSSELS & TOMATO 50

CLASSIC FETTUCCINE ALFREDO 51

PENNE WITH BROCCOLI, AGED CHEDDAR & BACON 52

ORECCHIETTE WITH WHITE ANCHOVIES & MINT 55

SPAGHETTI WITH TOMATO, FRESH MOZZARELLA & BASIL 56

SHELLS WITH TUNA, CHICKPEAS & PARSLEY 58

CLASSIC SPAGHETTI CARBONARA 59

WITH AS MUCH PASTA as I cook and eat, you'd swear that I was the full-blooded Italian chef on *The Chew* and not Mario Batali.

But of all the different categories of *5 in 5* cooking, pasta is definitely the one I cook and enjoy most. Starting with just a few pantry staples and a handful of fresh, seasonal ingredients, there is almost no limit to the range of possible dishes. In fact, I could write an entire *5 in 5* cookbook of nothing other than pasta recipes.

When it comes to the big debate of fresh versus dried pasta, there are cases to be made for each. The good news is that I truly enjoy the flavor and texture of both, so there really is no downside. Dried pasta is more convenient, capable of sitting forever on the shelf until it's needed. Fresh, on the other hand, must be refrigerated and, even then, it won't last too long. Dried pasta can take up to ten times as long to cook, so it definitely loses out to fresh in the timesaving department. But it is the much more economical choice.

For this book, I've treated dried pasta as a pantry staple and fresh pasta as a fresh ingredient. But when you make these recipes, feel free to swap dried for fresh and vice versa. When cooking dried pasta, I always undercut the time listed on the box by at least 1 minute. The goal is to end up with a firm not mushy noodle. When cooking fresh, have everything else ready to go because it finishes cooking in as little as a minute or two.

Last, never oversauce your pasta dishes. There is a good reason why this section is titled "Pasta" and not "Sauce"—the real star of the dish should always be the noodle. Think of the sauce much like the dressing for a salad. Less is almost always more.

I make this pasta at least once a week because I always have the ingredients on hand. It's quick, classic, and delicious—and I don't have to run to the store every time I want to make it. Pair it with a simply dressed arugula salad (OK, and maybe some garlic bread), and you have a great midweek meal.

ANGEL HAIR WITH TOMATOES & GARLIC

Serves 4

Kosher salt

1 pound dried angel hair pasta

3 tablespoons olive oil

3 **GARLIC** cloves, sliced

1 (28-ounce) can crushed San Marzano tomatoes with juices

1 tablespoon crushed red pepper flakes

1 tablespoon **UNSALTED BUTTER**

¼ cup **FRESH FLAT-LEAF PARSLEY** leaves, chopped

½ cup freshly grated **PARMESAN** cheese

1 In a very large pot, bring 5 quarts water and 3 tablespoons salt to a boil. Add the pasta and cook until just al dente, about 1 minute less than the package directions. Occasionally give the pasta a stir so it doesn't stick together. Scoop out and reserve 1 cup of the pasta water before draining the pasta.

2 Meanwhile, put a large skillet over low heat. Add the olive oil, garlic, and a pinch of salt. Cook until the garlic becomes aromatic, about 1 minute. Add the tomatoes with juices and red pepper flakes, increase the heat to medium-high, and cook for 2 minutes.

3 Add the cooked pasta to the pan, stirring the noodles into the sauce. Add a splash or two of the pasta water if the sauce looks too dry. Remove from the heat and stir in the butter, parsley, and Parmesan. Serve immediately.

Kosher salt

1 pound dried angel hair pasta

½ pound diced **PANCETTA** or bacon

2 **GARLIC** cloves, minced

1 cup fresh or frozen **PEAS**

½ cup torn **FRESH MINT** leaves

½ cup freshly grated **PARMESAN** cheese, or more
  to taste

3 tablespoons extra-virgin olive oil

In spring, sweet garden peas are at their peak of flavor—and I make every effort to incorporate them into my recipes, like this one. For good reason, peas and pancetta are a classic pairing: a duet of sweet and salty. Sure, you can substitute frozen peas if fresh aren't in season, but I'd rather wait until April or May and celebrate their arrival with this light, spring-y pasta.

ANGEL HAIR WITH PEAS & PANCETTA

Serves 4

1 In a very large pot, bring 5 quarts water and 3 tablespoons salt to a boil. Add the pasta and cook until just al dente, about 1 minute less than the package directions. Occasionally give the pasta a stir so it doesn't stick together. Scoop out and reserve 1 cup of the pasta water before draining the pasta.

2 Meanwhile, put a large skillet over medium heat. Add the pancetta and cook until almost crisp, about 3 minutes. Don't drain off the fat. Add the garlic to the pan and stir, making sure it doesn't brown, for 30 seconds.

3 Add the reserved pasta water and the peas. Simmer for 1 minute.

4 Add the cooked pasta to the pan, stirring the noodles into the sauce, and cook for 30 seconds. Remove from the heat and stir in the mint, Parmesan, and olive oil. Taste and adjust the seasoning, adding additional Parmesan if desired. Serve immediately.

In late summer and early fall, cauliflower is beautiful, plentiful, and cheap—and that's when you'll find me making this pasta. Because this dish is on the heartier side, it works great in cooler weather, too. Something magical happens to cauliflower when it is caramelized in a hot pan: It gets sweeter, nuttier, more complex. To ensure a quick and consistent sauté, cut the florets into very small pieces.

CAVATELLI WITH CAULIFLOWER & RED PEPPER FLAKES

Serves 4

Kosher salt and freshly ground black pepper

1 pound FRESH CAVATELLI pasta

¼ cup olive oil

1 small YELLOW ONION, thinly sliced (1 cup)

5 cups small CAULIFLOWER florets (from 1 large head)

2 WHITE ANCHOVIES, minced

½ tablespoon crushed red pepper flakes

1 cup freshly grated PARMESAN cheese

2 tablespoons extra-virgin olive oil

1 In a very large pot, bring 5 quarts water and 3 tablespoons salt to a boil. Add the pasta and cook until just al dente, about 1 minute less than the package directions. Occasionally give the pasta a stir so it doesn't stick together. Scoop out and reserve 1 cup of the pasta water before draining the pasta.

2 Meanwhile, put a large skillet over medium-high heat. Add the olive oil, onion, cauliflower, and anchovies and cook, stirring occasionally, until the mixture begins to caramelize, about 3 minutes. Taste and adjust the seasoning, adding salt and black pepper as needed.

3 Add the red pepper flakes and reserved pasta water and deglaze the pan, scraping with a wooden spoon to get up the browned bits on the bottom of the pan. Add the cooked pasta to the pan, stirring it into the sauce. Cook for 1 minute. Remove from the heat and stir in the Parmesan and extra-virgin olive oil. Serve immediately.

This recipe is all about fresh, juicy, ripe tomatoes—preferably heirloom varieties straight from your garden or the local farmers' market. If you happen to have some squishy, over-ripe tomatoes, go ahead and use them here. Thanks to the addition of nice and smoky bacon, this dish is like the pasta version of a BLT. My nephew Henry is obsessed both with gardening and bacon, so this is one of our favorite things to make together.

ANGEL HAIR WITH BACON & TOMATOES

Serves 4

Kosher salt and freshly ground black pepper

1 pound dried angel hair pasta

2 tablespoons olive oil

1 cup diced **BACON**

3 **GARLIC** cloves, sliced

3 cups medium-diced **TOMATOES**

½ cup freshly grated **PARMESAN** cheese

½ cup torn **FRESH BASIL** leaves

2 tablespoons extra-virgin olive oil

1 In a very large pot, bring 5 quarts water and 3 tablespoons salt to a boil. Add the pasta and cook until just al dente, about 1 minute less than the package directions. Occasionally give the pasta a stir so it doesn't stick together. Scoop out and reserve 1 cup of the pasta water before draining the pasta.

2 Meanwhile, put a large skillet over medium heat. Add the olive oil and bacon and cook until almost crisp, about 3 minutes. Don't drain off the bacon fat. Add the garlic and cook for about 30 seconds, making sure it doesn't get too brown. Add the tomatoes and increase the heat to medium-high.

3 Add the pasta and reserved pasta water to the pan, stirring the noodles into the sauce. Remove from the heat and stir in the Parmesan, basil, and extra-virgin olive oil. Taste and adjust the seasoning, adding salt and pepper as needed. Serve immediately.

I know it's not the cool chef-thing to say, but I still love good-old button mushrooms—and have since I was a kid. They're inexpensive, easy to find, and available all year long. To get the most out of these humble fungi, quarter and caramelize them well, which intensifies their woodsy flavor. If you want to get a little fancy and don't mind spending a few more bucks, you can swap wild mushrooms like chanterelles or hen-of-the-woods to make the dish a little more special.

ORECCHIETTE WITH MUSHROOMS, SPINACH & GOAT CHEESE

Serves 4

Kosher salt and freshly ground black pepper

1 pound **FRESH ORECCHIETTE** pasta

2 tablespoons olive oil, or more if needed

3 cups quartered **BUTTON MUSHROOMS** (from 8 ounces)

4 cups roughly chopped **BABY SPINACH**

8 ounces fresh **GOAT CHEESE**

1 In a very large pot, bring 5 quarts water and 3 tablespoons salt to a boil. Add the pasta and cook until just al dente, about 1 minute less than the package directions. Occasionally give the pasta a stir so it doesn't stick together. Scoop out and reserve 1 cup of the pasta water before draining the pasta.

2 Meanwhile, put a large skillet over medium-high heat. Add the olive oil and mushrooms, spreading them out into an even layer on the bottom of the pan. Cook, stirring occasionally, until well browned, about 3 minutes. If the pan looks dry, add up to an additional 2 tablespoons olive oil. Add the spinach and a pinch of salt and give the mixture a quick stir.

3 Add the reserved pasta water. Remove from the heat and stir in the goat cheese until fully incorporated. Add the cooked pasta to the pan, stirring the noodles into the sauce. Taste and adjust the seasoning, adding salt and pepper as needed. Serve immediately.

If you've watched me on *The Chew*, you've probably heard me say how much I love Ohio sweet corn. If you haven't: I LOVE OHIO SWEET CORN! While corn might not be a traditional Italian ingredient, it does happen to go great with pasta, especially when paired with the sweet-and-salty punch of ripe tomatoes and crumbled feta. And trust me: If Italy had corn as sweet as we do in Ohio, it would be a staple in that country too!

ANGEL HAIR WITH CORN, FETA & TOMATO

Serves 4

Kosher salt

1 pound dried angel hair pasta

3 tablespoons olive oil

3 ears SWEET CORN, kernels cut from the cobs (about 2 cups)

2 GARLIC cloves, sliced

3 tablespoons FRESH OREGANO leaves

½ tablespoon crushed red pepper flakes

2 cups GRAPE TOMATOES, halved

2 tablespoons extra-virgin olive oil

1 cup crumbled FETA cheese

1 In a very large pot, bring 5 quarts water and 3 tablespoons salt to a boil. Add the pasta and cook until just al dente, about 1 minute less than the package directions. Occasionally give the pasta a stir so it doesn't stick together. Scoop out and reserve 1 cup of the pasta water before draining the pasta.

2 Meanwhile, put a large skillet over medium-high heat. Add the olive oil and corn, spreading the kernels out into an even layer on the bottom of the pan. Let the kernels cook, without stirring, until browned, about 2 minutes. Reduce the heat to medium and add the garlic, oregano, and a good pinch of salt. Cook until aromatic, about 1 minute.

3 Stir in the red pepper flakes, add the reserved pasta water, and cook for 1 minute.

4 Add the cooked pasta to the pan, stirring the noodles into the sauce. Remove from the heat and stir in the tomatoes, extra-virgin olive oil, and feta. Serve immediately.

This recipe highlights how just a few basic ingredients can come together to create something special. Because there are so few elements, it's important to use fresh herbs, plump and firm garlic, and the best-quality Parmesan you can get your hands on. This recipe works equally well with shellfish, so feel free to add shrimp, scallops, or even lobster if you're feeling adventurous.

SPAGHETTI WITH OLIVE OIL, GARLIC & RED PEPPER FLAKES

Serves 4

Kosher salt and freshly ground black pepper

1 pound dried spaghetti

¼ cup olive oil

5 GARLIC cloves, sliced

1 tablespoon crushed red pepper flakes

½ cup FRESH FLAT-LEAF PARSLEY leaves, chopped

½ cup freshly grated PARMESAN cheese

1 tablespoon UNSALTED BUTTER

1 In a very large pot, bring 5 quarts water and 3 tablespoons salt to a boil. Add the pasta and cook until just al dente, about 1 minute less than the package directions. Occasionally give the pasta a stir so it doesn't stick together. Scoop out and reserve 1 cup of the pasta water before draining the pasta.

2 Meanwhile, put a large skillet over low heat. Add the olive oil and garlic and cook until the garlic is soft and aromatic, about 3 minutes. Add the red pepper flakes along with the reserved pasta water to the garlic. Increase the heat to medium and bring the mixture to a simmer.

3 Add the cooked pasta to the pan, stirring the noodles into the sauce. Taste and adjust the seasoning, adding salt and black pepper as needed.

4 Remove from the heat and stir in the parsley, Parmesan, and butter. Serve immediately.

When people think of meat sauce, they wrongly assume that it has to be an all-day process. Don't get me wrong—I love the authentic, slow-simmered classic, but I don't always have the time to make it. This recipe is a lightning-quick version of Bolognese that satisfies both my busy schedule and my meat-loving bones!

TAGLIATELLE WITH QUICK MEAT SAUCE

Serves 4

Kosher salt

1 pound FRESH TAGLIATELLE pasta

1 tablespoon olive oil

1 pound GROUND BEEF (90% lean)

1 small YELLOW ONION, diced (about 1 cup)

1 (14-ounce) can diced San Marzano tomatoes with juices

¼ cup FRESH OREGANO leaves, roughly chopped

½ tablespoon crushed red pepper flakes

1 cup freshly grated PARMESAN cheese, or more to taste

1 In a very large pot, bring 5 quarts water and 3 tablespoons salt to a boil. Add the pasta and cook until just al dente, about 1 minute less than the package directions. Occasionally give the pasta a stir so it doesn't stick together. Reserve ½ cup of the pasta water before draining the pasta.

2 Meanwhile, put a large skillet over medium-high heat. Add the olive oil and then the ground beef and a pinch of salt. Cook, stirring with a wooden spoon to break up the meat, until browned, about 2 minutes. Scoot the beef to one side of the pan, add the onion and a pinch of salt to the empty space, and cook for 1 minute.

3 Add the reserved pasta water and deglaze the pan, scraping with a wooden spoon to get up the browned bits on the bottom of the pan. Add the tomatoes with juices, oregano, and red pepper flakes and bring to a simmer.

4 Stir the pasta into the sauce in the pan. Remove from the heat and stir in the Parmesan. Taste and adjust the seasoning, adding additional Parmesan if desired. Serve immediately.

This pasta is very similar to Tagliatelle with Quick Meat Sauce (opposite), but by substituting spicy chorizo sausage for ground beef, you give the dish some zesty Latin flair. It's pretty easy these days to find fresh (not cured) chorizo at the supermarket or Mexican grocery, but if you can't, go ahead and substitute spicy Italian sausage. Using San Marzano tomatoes, which are canned when sweet and ripe, really makes a difference in a simple recipe like this.

RIGATONI WITH CHORIZO & MANCHEGO

Serves 4

Kosher salt

1 pound **FRESH RIGATONI** pasta

1 tablespoons olive oil

1 pound **FRESH CHORIZO**, removed from casings if not bulk

1 small **YELLOW ONION**, diced (about 1 cup)

½ cup dry **WHITE WINE**

1 (28-ounce) can diced San Marzano tomatoes with juices

2 tablespoons extra-virgin olive oil

1 cup freshly grated **MANCHEGO** cheese, or more to taste

1 In a very large pot, bring 5 quarts water and 3 tablespoons salt to a boil. Add the pasta and cook until just al dente, about 1 minute less than the package directions. Occasionally give the pasta a stir so it doesn't stick together. Drain.

2 Meanwhile, put a large skillet over medium heat. Add the olive oil and then the chorizo. Cook, stirring with a wooden spoon to break up the meat, until browned, about 2 minutes. Scoot the chorizo to one side of the pan, add the onion and a pinch of salt to the empty space, and cook for 1 minute. Add the white wine and deglaze the pan, scraping with a wooden spoon to get up the browned bits on the bottom of the pan. Cook until reduced by half, about 1 minute. Add the tomatoes with juices and bring to a simmer. Taste and adjust the seasoning, adding more salt as needed.

3 Add the cooked pasta to the pan, stirring it into the sauce. Remove from the heat and stir in the extra-virgin olive oil and Manchego. Garnish with more cheese if desired. Serve immediately.

Kosher salt

1 pound **FRESH ORECCHIETTE** pasta

2 tablespoons olive oil

½ pound **SPICY ITALIAN SAUSAGE**, removed from the casings if not bulk

4 cups roughly chopped **KALE** leaves (stem before chopping)

½ cup freshly grated **PARMESAN** cheese, or more to taste

2 tablespoons extra-virgin olive oil

This is my wife Lizzie's and my favorite pasta dish: If we see it on a restaurant menu, we order it. If it's a little chilly outside and we're staying in, we make it—it's that good! Kale is a hearty, leafy green that really stands up to zesty sausage, and it tastes best in fall and winter when it's a touch sweeter. If you don't like spicy food, you can substitute mild sausage or even chicken sausage. (Confession: This recipe might require closer to 6 minutes, but it's worth it!)

ORECCHIETTE WITH SAUSAGE & KALE

Serves 4

1 In a very large pot, bring 5 quarts water and 3 tablespoons salt to a boil. Add the pasta and cook until just al dente, about 1 minute less than the package directions. Occasionally give the pasta a stir so it doesn't stick together. Scoop out and reserve 1 cup of the pasta water before draining the pasta.

2 Meanwhile, put large skillet over medium-high heat. Add the olive oil. When the oil is hot, add the sausage and cook, stirring only occasionally, until very well browned, about 4 minutes. Add the kale and cook for 1 minute, stirring constantly.

3 Add the reserved pasta water and deglaze the pan, scraping with a wooden spoon to get up the browned bits on the bottom of the pan. Add the cooked pasta to the pan, stirring the noodles into the sauce.

4 Remove from the heat and stir in the Parmesan and extra-virgin olive oil. Taste and adjust the seasoning, adding additional Parmesan if desired. Serve immediately.

This is a no-bake macaroni and cheese dish that still delivers all the rich and creamy goodness of more complicated recipes in a fraction of the time. I can't understand why people still make the boxed stuff when you can make it from scratch in the same amount of time. Feel free to try using other cheeses, too. This version does sacrifice the crusty, breaded topping of baked casseroles, but it's ready to enjoy in a flash and just as comforting. (And if you really miss that topping, see the note at the end.)

NO-BAKE MAC & CHEESE

Serves 4

Kosher salt and freshly ground black pepper

1 pound **FRESH RIGATONI** pasta

2 cups **HEAVY CREAM**

1 teaspoon hot sauce, or to taste

½ cup **MASCARPONE** (if you cannot find it, cream cheese will work in a pinch)

1 cup grated **AGED CHEDDAR** cheese

½ cup finely chopped **FRESH CHIVES**

1 In a very large pot, bring 5 quarts water and 3 tablespoons salt to a boil. Add the pasta and cook until just al dente, about 1 minute less than the package directions. Occasionally give the pasta a stir so it doesn't stick together. Drain.

2 Meanwhile, put a 2-quart saucepan or Dutch oven over medium heat. Add the cream, hot sauce, 1 teaspoon salt, and pepper to taste and bring to a simmer. Cook until the cream has reduced by one-third, about 3 minutes. Add the mascarpone and cheddar, whisking to incorporate them into the cream.

3 When the cheeses are fully melted and blended into the sauce, add the cooked pasta and chives, stirring them into the sauce. Serve immediately.

NOTE: To add a crunchy topping, spread a layer of panko or plain dry bread crumbs on top and put under a hot broiler until golden brown, about 1 minute.

Kosher salt and freshly ground black pepper

1 pound FRESH PAPPARDELLE pasta

3 tablespoons olive oil

4 cups sliced BUTTON MUSHROOMS (from
   1 pound)

1 small RED ONION, thinly sliced (1 cup)

¾ cup SOUR CREAM

¼ cup FRESH TARRAGON leaves, roughly
   chopped

This filling and satisfying pasta is finished with sour cream, which creates a rich, creamy sauce. And as the sauce simmers, it picks up the deep, woodsy mushroom flavors. But the addition of fresh and fragrant tarragon keeps the dish bright and lively. Warning: You may feel like taking a nap—or hitting the gym—after this meal.

PAPPARDELLE WITH MUSHROOM CREAM SAUCE

Serves 4

1 In a very large pot, bring 5 quarts water and 3 tablespoons salt to a boil. Add the pasta and cook until just al dente, about 1 minute less than the package directions. Occasionally give the pasta a stir so it doesn't stick together. Scoop out and reserve 1 cup of the pasta water before draining the pasta.

2 Meanwhile, put a large skillet over medium-high heat. Add the olive oil, mushrooms, and onion along with a pinch of salt. Cook until the vegetables are slightly caramelized, about 3 minutes.

3 Add the reserved pasta water and deglaze the pan, scraping with a wooden spoon to get up the browned bits on the bottom of the pan. Cook until the sauce is reduced by half, about 2 minutes. Add the sour cream and tarragon, stirring to fully incorporate. Taste and adjust the seasoning, adding salt and pepper if needed.

4 Add the cooked pasta to the pan, stirring it into the sauce. Serve immediately.

Kosher salt

1 pound dried spaghetti

1 tablespoon olive oil

1 pound **MUSSELS**, cleaned

1 **JALAPEÑO**, thinly sliced (optional)

5 **GARLIC** cloves, sliced

¾ cup dry **WHITE WINE**

1 (14-ounce) can crushed San Marzano tomatoes with juices

1 cup **FRESH BASIL** leaves, torn

3 tablespoons extra-virgin olive oil

I love using mussels in pasta recipes because they add that special-occasion feel while still being easy to find, easy to cook, and easy on the wallet. Plus, their toothsome texture satisfies my taste for meat at times, like Lent, when I typically don't eat it. Before cooking with mussels, make sure they are tightly closed (if they are slightly ajar, tap them on the counter and see if they close). An open mussel is likely a dead mussel and therefore not safe to eat.

SPAGHETTI WITH MUSSELS & TOMATO

Serves 4

1 In a very large pot, bring 5 quarts water and 3 tablespoons salt to a boil. Add the pasta and cook until just al dente, about 1 minute less than the package directions. Occasionally give the pasta a stir so it doesn't stick together. Drain.

2 Meanwhile, put a large Dutch oven over medium-high heat. Add the olive oil followed by the mussels, jalapeño, garlic, and a pinch of salt. Cover the pot and cook for 1 minute.

3 Pour in the white wine and deglaze the pan, scraping with a wooden spoon to get up the browned bits on the bottom of the pan. Re-cover and cook for 1 minute. Add the tomatoes with juices and bring to a simmer uncovered. Taste and adjust the seasoning, adding salt as needed.

4 If all the mussels haven't yet opened, cook for another minute or so. (Discard any that still do not open.) Add the cooked pasta to the pan, stirring the noodles into the sauce. Remove from the heat and stir in the basil and extra-virgin olive oil. Serve immediately.

Kosher salt and freshly ground black pepper

1 pound FRESH FETTUCCINE pasta

8 tablespoons (1 stick) UNSALTED BUTTER

1½ cups freshly grated PARMESAN cheese

Many of us have come to know Fettuccine Alfredo as a thick and gooey pasta swimming in a bland cream sauce. *Wrong!* The authentic version uses no cream at all, instead relying on good-quality butter and cheese—loosened a bit with pasta water—to achieve a delicately seductive sauce. And no surprise here: The real version tastes better, is easier to make, and costs less!

CLASSIC FETTUCCINE ALFREDO

Serves 4

1 In a very large pot, bring 5 quarts water and 3 tablespoons salt to a boil. Add the pasta and cook until just al dente, about 1 minute less than the package directions. Occasionally give the pasta a stir so it doesn't stick together. Scoop out and reserve 1 cup of the pasta water before draining the pasta.

2 Put a large skillet over medium heat. Add the reserved pasta water to the pan and bring to a simmer. Whisk in the butter and 1 cup of the Parmesan and return to a simmer. Add the cooked pasta and remaining ½ cup cheese, stirring the noodles into the sauce.

3 Taste and adjust the seasoning, adding salt and pepper as needed. Serve immediately.

Kosher salt

1 pound FRESH PENNE pasta

1 tablespoon olive oil

½ pound BACON, diced

4 cups small BROCCOLI florets (from 1 large head)

¾ cup PINE NUTS

1½ cups shredded AGED CHEDDAR cheese, or more to taste

1 teaspoon crushed red pepper flakes

Okay, I'll admit it: This pasta has *zero* Italian pedigree. But my nephews love it just the same, and I am powerless to resist them. This dish is like the pasta version of broccoli with cheese sauce— and it's a great way to get kids to eat their veggies! Cut the florets small so they cook up quickly. I freeze the bigger stems to use later in broccoli soup.

PENNE WITH BROCCOLI, AGED CHEDDAR & BACON

Serves 4

1 In a very large pot, bring 5 quarts water and 3 tablespoons salt to a boil. Add the pasta and cook until just al dente, about 1 minute less than the package directions. Occasionally give the pasta a stir so it doesn't stick together. Scoop out and reserve 1 cup of the pasta water before draining the pasta.

2 Meanwhile, put a large skillet over medium-high heat. Add the olive oil and then the bacon. Cook until the bacon is almost crisp, about 2 minutes. Add the broccoli and pine nuts and cook until the pine nuts are light golden brown and the bacon is fully crisp, about 1 minute.

3 Add the reserved pasta water and deglaze the pan, scraping with a wooden spoon to get up the browned bits on the bottom of the pan. Cook for 1 minute.

4 Reduce the heat to low and stir in the cheddar and red pepper flakes. When the cheese is melted and fully incorporated, add the cooked pasta to the pan, stirring it into the sauce. Serve immediately, topping with more cheddar if desired.

While on vacation in Italy with family and friends, I was planning to cook a fancy pasta dish using fresh-caught sea urchin. But when we went to the market, there was no sea urchin in sight. So I quickly improvised, grabbing some briny, beautiful white anchovies instead. What started out as a huge disappointment ended up being one of our favorite pasta dishes on the trip—and made birthday girl Stephanie March pretty happy, too.

ORECCHIETTE WITH WHITE ANCHOVIES & MINT

Serves 4

Kosher salt

1 pound **FRESH ORECCHIETTE** pasta

6 tablespoons olive oil

4 ounces **WHITE ANCHOVIES**, minced

½ tablespoon crushed red pepper flakes

¾ cup torn **FRESH MINT** leaves

½ cup freshly grated **PARMESAN** cheese

3 tablespoons **UNSALTED BUTTER**

1 In a very large pot, bring 5 quarts water and 3 tablespoons salt to a boil. Add the pasta and cook until just al dente, about 1 minute less than the package directions. Occasionally give the pasta a stir so it doesn't stick together. Scoop out and reserve 1 cup of the pasta water before draining the pasta.

2 Meanwhile, put a large skillet over low heat. Add the olive oil and then the anchovies and red pepper flakes. Cook, stirring occasionally, for 4 minutes.

3 Increase the heat to medium-high and add the reserved pasta water, stirring vigorously to blend the mixture. Add the cooked pasta to the pan, stirring it into the sauce.

4 Remove from the heat and stir in the mint, Parmesan, and butter. Serve immediately.

This recipe is tailor-made for summer because it uses a ton of ripe tomatoes and fragrant basil in an uncooked sauce that preserves the tastes of the season (without heating up the kitchen). When Lizzie and I are looking for a light, fresh, and summery pasta dish, this is the one we often gravitate to. Go ahead and make the tomato mixture ahead of time and let it sit at room temperature if you'd like. Serve with some good crusty bread.

SPAGHETTI WITH TOMATO, FRESH MOZZARELLA & BASIL

Serves 4

Kosher salt and freshly ground black pepper

1 pound dried spaghetti

½ cup olive oil

5 **GARLIC** cloves, sliced

4 cups diced **TOMATOES** (from 1 pound)

3 cups large-diced **FRESH MOZZARELLA** cheese (from 1 pound)

2 cups **FRESH BASIL** leaves, torn

½ cup fresh bread crumbs

5 tablespoons freshly grated **PARMESAN** cheese

1 In a very large pot, bring 5 quarts water and 3 tablespoons salt to a boil. Add the pasta and cook until just al dente, about 1 minute less than the package directions. Occasionally give the pasta a stir so it doesn't stick together. Scoop out and reserve ½ cup of the pasta water before draining the pasta.

2 Meanwhile, put a large skillet over low heat. Add ¼ cup of the olive oil followed by the garlic. Cook until the garlic becomes fragrant but not browned, about 1 minute.

3 In a large bowl, combine the tomatoes, mozzarella, and 1½ cups of the basil. Season generously with salt and pepper.

4 Add the cooked pasta and reserved pasta water to the garlic in the pan and cook for 1 minute. Taste and adjust the seasoning, adding salt and pepper as needed. Pour into the bowl with the tomatoes and mozzarella, stirring to combine.

5 Meanwhile, put a small skillet over medium heat. Add the remaining ¼ cup olive oil and the bread crumbs. Cook until golden brown, about 2 minutes. Remove from the heat and stir in the Parmesan.

6 Garnish the pasta with the bread crumb mixture and remaining ½ cup basil and serve immediately.

When I was fresh out of culinary school, I lived with a couple of my best childhood buddies. One of them, Ted Baugh, my good friend to this day, practically lived on Tuna Noodle Casserole—so much so that the smell still haunts me. This is an updated, slightly more elegant version that features good-quality jarred tuna and comes together in a jiff. Teddy, this one's for you!

SHELLS WITH TUNA, CHICKPEAS & PARSLEY

Serves 4

Kosher salt and freshly ground black pepper

1 pound dried small pasta shells

1 (7-ounce) jar OLIVE OIL–PACKED TUNA (Tonnino is my favorite)

2 GARLIC cloves, minced

½ tablespoon crushed red pepper flakes

1 cup drained cooked CHICKPEAS (canned is fine)

1 cup FRESH FLAT-LEAF PARSLEY leaves, chopped

Grated zest and juice of 1 LEMON

2 tablespoons extra-virgin olive oil

1 In a very large pot, bring 5 quarts water and 3 tablespoons salt to a boil. Add the pasta and cook until just al dente, about 1 minute less than the package directions. Occasionally give the pasta a stir so it doesn't stick together. Scoop out and reserve 1 cup of the pasta water before draining the pasta.

2 Meanwhile, put a 2-quart Dutch oven over low heat. Add the tuna and the oil it was packed in to the pan, stirring with a wooden spoon to break it up. Add the garlic, red pepper flakes, and chickpeas and cook for 3 minutes. Season with salt and black pepper.

3 Add the reserved pasta water and increase the heat to medium-high. Gently stir to bring the sauce together.

4 Add the cooked pasta to the pan, stirring the noodles into the sauce. Taste and adjust the seasoning, adding salt and black pepper as needed. Remove from the heat and stir in the parsley, lemon zest and juice, and olive oil. Serve immediately.

This is another one of those pasta dishes that really has strayed from its classic preparation by growing richer, creamer, and heavier. The *real* version is like bacon and eggs on pasta, but with guanciale (cured pork jowl) instead of bacon. If you can't find guanciale, go ahead and use good-quality bacon or pancetta. By separating the eggs and mixing the yolk into the pasta at the last minute, you end up with a rich and silky texture. One quick note: Be sure those eggs are extra-fresh and serve this dish only to those in tip-top form. The egg will be warmed by the hot pasta, but it's not going to cook fully.

CLASSIC SPAGHETTI CARBONARA

Serves 4

Kosher salt

1 pound dried spaghetti

4 tablespoons olive oil

½ pound GUANCIALE, cut into small dice

4 LARGE EGGS, separated

1 teaspoon freshly ground black pepper

¼ cup chopped FRESH FLAT-LEAF PARSLEY leaves

1 cup freshly grated PARMESAN cheese

1 In a very large pot, bring 5 quarts water and 3 tablespoons salt to a boil. Add the pasta and cook until just al dente, about 1 minute less than the package directions. Occasionally give the pasta a stir so it doesn't stick together. Scoop out and reserve ¼ cup of the pasta water before draining the pasta.

2 Meanwhile, put a large skillet over medium-high heat. Add 1 tablespoon of the olive oil and then the guanciale and cook until the meat is almost crisp, about 3 minutes. Add the reserved pasta water and deglaze the pan, scraping with a wooden spoon to get up the browned bits on the bottom of the pan. Turn off the heat.

3 Whisk the egg whites until they start to get foamy. Add the pepper, parsley, remaining 3 tablespoons olive oil, and the Parmesan. Add this egg white mixture to the pan with the guanciale, stirring vigorously to incorporate and being careful to not scramble the eggs. Taste and adjust the seasoning, adding salt and pepper as needed.

4 Add the cooked pasta to the pan, stirring the noodles into the sauce. Divide the pasta among 4 bowls, topping each portion with an egg yolk. Serve immediately, allowing diners to mix the yolk into the pasta at the table for that extra dose of decadence!

PORK TENDERLOIN WITH SOY, GINGER & CILANTRO 63

SIRLOIN WITH LEMON & OREGANO 64

BEEF SATAY WITH CILANTRO PESTO 65

CHICKEN SATAY WITH SPICY PEANUT SAUCE 66

LAZY MEATBALL KEBABS WITH YOGURT 69

LAMB SAUSAGE KEBABS WITH TOMATO 70

CHICKEN WITH SPICY YOGURT & CILANTRO 71

SHRIMP WITH PINEAPPLE GLAZE 72

2 ON A STICK

IS IT JUST ME or does everything taste better when cooked and served on a stick?! I'm not sure if it's my Greek heritage or my undying love for street food, but I can't seem to get enough kebabs.

You can definitely cook kebabs year round, especially if you live in a moderate climate—or are using a grill pan on the stove. But I typically reserve these recipes for summer, when friends and family can keep me company in the backyard around the grill. And when it comes to large crowds, nothing beats big platters of kebabs for ease of cooking and cleanup. You don't even need any silverware! When cooking for a crowd, you can certainly pick one or more of the recipes in this chapter. But I suggest you put out a selection of meats, veggies, and sauces and let your guests design their own kebabs.

If you are using wooden skewers, make sure you soak them for at least 30 minutes in salt water to keep them from catching fire on the grill. The salt acts to season the meat from the inside while cooking. Neat, huh?

As I always say when it comes to recipes: You should use them as an instructive guide, not a bible. And nowhere does that rule apply more than when cooking on a stick. Take these basic ideas and let your mind run wild.

Because pork tenderloin is so lean, it really benefits from a quick and flavorful marinade. The ginger and soy give this dish a little Asian flair, the honey a touch of sweetness, and the cilantro adds a summery brightness.

PORK TENDERLOIN WITH SOY, GINGER & CILANTRO

Makes 6 skewers; serves 6

¼ cup soy sauce

¼ cup olive oil

2 tablespoons honey

Grated zest and juice of 2 **LIMES**

2 tablespoons finely grated peeled **FRESH GINGER**

1 **GARLIC** clove, minced

2 (1-pound) **PORK TENDERLOINS**, cut into 1-inch cubes (have your butcher do this)

Kosher salt and freshly ground black pepper

¼ cup roughly chopped **FRESH CILANTRO** leaves

1 Preheat a grill or grill pan to medium-high heat.

2 In a medium bowl, whisk together the soy sauce, olive oil, honey, lime zest and juice, ginger, and garlic. Season the pork with salt and pepper. Toss the pork in the marinade before threading 6 pieces of pork onto each of 6 skewers.

3 Put the skewers on the grill, cover, and cook until the meat is well caramelized, about 2 minutes per side.

4 Remove the skewers from the grill and put them on a platter. Top with the chopped cilantro and serve immediately.

I grew up eating kebabs like these. Whenever my mom cooked beef, oregano and lemon were usually involved. For those of you who love (overpriced, in my opinion) beef tenderloin, go ahead and give sirloin—and this recipe—a try. The meat has better texture and better flavor, and it costs less. What? Are you going to disagree with my mom?

SIRLOIN WITH LEMON & OREGANO

Makes 6 skewers; serves 6

1½ pounds **BEEF SIRLOIN**, cut into 1-inch cubes (have your butcher do this)

Kosher salt and freshly ground black pepper

Grated zest and juice of 2 **LEMONS**

2 tablespoons chopped **FRESH OREGANO** leaves

2 **GARLIC** cloves, minced

1 teaspoon coriander seeds, toasted and ground

6 tablespoons extra-virgin olive oil

4 cups loosely packed **ARUGULA**

1 Preheat a grill or grill pan to medium-high heat.

2 Thread 6 pieces of sirloin onto each of 6 skewers and season well with salt and pepper.

3 In a medium bowl, whisk together the lemon zest and juice, oregano, garlic, coriander, and olive oil. Divide this vinaigrette equally between 2 bowls, a small one for basting the meat, and a larger one for dressing the arugula.

4 Liberally brush the skewered meat with the vinaigrette baste and put the skewers on the grill. Cover and cook until the meat is well caramelized, about 2 minutes per side. Baste liberally with the vinaigrette while cooking.

5 Remove the skewers from the grill and put them on a platter. Toss the arugula with the remaining vinaigrette and mound on top of the skewers. Serve immediately.

Liz and I keep a pretty large garden at home, and by midsummer the cilantro just goes wild. I like to cut it way back and make big batches of this amazing pesto, which is a nice alternative to the usual basil variety. I freeze it into ice cube trays and then pop the cubes into freezer bags so I always have some around. Use it on beef, chicken, and even fish.

BEEF SATAY WITH CILANTRO PESTO

Makes 8 skewers; serves 4

2 tablespoons olive oil

1 teaspoon coriander seeds, toasted and ground

½ teaspoon crushed red pepper flakes

1 pound BEEF SIRLOIN, cut into 1-inch cubes (have your butcher do this)

Kosher salt and freshly ground black pepper

2 cups FRESH CILANTRO leaves

2 GARLIC cloves, roughly chopped

¼ cup roughly chopped TOASTED HAZELNUTS

½ cup freshly grated PARMESAN cheese

½ cup extra-virgin olive oil

1 Preheat a grill or grill pan to medium-high heat.

2 In a medium bowl, whisk together the olive oil, coriander, and red pepper flakes. Season the beef with salt and black pepper. Add the beef pieces to the marinade and toss to coat. Divide the beef into 8 portions and thread the meat onto each of 8 skewers.

3 Put the beef skewers on the grill, cover, and cook for 3 minutes. Flip the beef, cover, and cook until the meat is well caramelized, about 2 minutes.

4 Meanwhile, in a blender or food processor, combine the cilantro, garlic, hazelnuts, Parmesan, and extra-virgin olive oil. Process until smooth. Taste and adjust the seasoning, adding salt as needed.

5 Remove the skewers from the grill and put on a platter. Drizzle with some of the cilantro pesto and serve the rest on the side as a dipping sauce. Serve immediately.

This recipe doesn't stray too far from the classic chicken satay that you'd find at a Thai restaurant. My stepson, Kyle, loves this dish—and he loves it "Thai hot." Don't worry; this version is toned down for the rest of us who don't have asbestos tongues.

CHICKEN SATAY WITH SPICY PEANUT SAUCE

Makes 8 skewers; serves 6 to 8

2 tablespoons **PEANUT BUTTER**

Grated zest and juice of 2 **ORANGES**

1 **JALAPEÑO**, minced

¼ cup soy sauce

¼ cup olive oil

8 (4-ounce) boneless, skinless **CHICKEN THIGHS** halved

Kosher salt and freshly ground black pepper

¼ cup roughly chopped **FRESH CILANTRO** leaves

1 Preheat a grill or grill pan to medium-high heat.

2 In a small bowl, whisk together the peanut butter, orange zest and juice, jalapeño, soy sauce, and olive oil. Season the chicken with salt and pepper. In a medium bowl, toss the chicken with half of the peanut sauce, mixing well to coat the meat.

3 Thread 2 pieces of chicken onto each of 8 skewers. Put the skewers on the grill, cover, and cook for 3 minutes. Flip the meat, cover, and cook until the meat is well caramelized, about 2 minutes.

4 Remove the skewers from the grill and put them on a platter. Drizzle with the remaining peanut sauce and top with the cilantro. Serve immediately.

Growing up, all my friends thought our family was weird because we dipped all of our grilled meats into yogurt. Now it's pretty common to use yogurt in all sorts of sauces—but the Greek in me thinks it still works best with grilled meat, preferably a kebab hot from the grill like this one.

LAZY MEATBALL KEBABS WITH YOGURT

Makes 8 skewers; serves 6 to 8

1½ pounds SPICY ITALIAN SAUSAGE, removed from casings if not bulk

Kosher salt and freshly ground black pepper

1 cup GREEK YOGURT

¼ cup extra-virgin olive oil

½ cup small-diced CUCUMBER

Grated zest and juice of 1 LEMON

¼ cup chopped FRESH MINT leaves

1 Preheat a grill or grill pan to medium-high heat.

2 Form the sausage into 16 small meatballs and thread 2 onto each of 8 skewers. Press the meatballs lightly with your hand to form them into patties. Season the meatballs with salt and pepper.

3 Put the skewers on the grill, cover, and cook for 3 minutes. Flip the skewers, cover, and cook until the meat is well caramelized, about 2 minutes.

4 Meanwhile, in a small bowl, whisk together the yogurt, olive oil, cucumber, lemon zest and juice, and mint. Taste and adjust the seasoning, adding salt and pepper if needed.

5 Remove the kebabs from the grill and put them on a platter. Serve with the yogurt sauce on the side. Serve immediately.

1 pound **LAMB SAUSAGE**, removed from casings if not bulk

Kosher salt and freshly ground black pepper

2 tablespoons olive oil

¼ cup extra-virgin olive oil

3 tablespoons red wine vinegar

1 large **TOMATO**, cut into small dice

½ cup thinly sliced **RED ONION**

½ cup torn **FRESH MINT** leaves

½ cup **GREEK YOGURT**

Although I almost always make my own sausage, there are still times that I'm just not in the mood to set up and then clean the grinder. Most good butchers sell a variety of house-made sausage that really speeds up the prep time for a weekday meal. If you haven't tried lamb sausage, you should. It's got a great gamey quality that is wonderful when grilled.

LAMB SAUSAGE KEBABS WITH TOMATO

Makes 6 skewers; serves 3

1 Preheat a grill or grill pan to medium-high heat.

2 Form the lamb sausage into 12 small meatballs and thread 2 onto each of 6 skewers. Press the meatballs lightly with your hand to form them into patties. Season the meatballs with salt and pepper and then drizzle with the olive oil.

3 Put the skewers on the grill, cover, and cook for 3 minutes. Flip the meat, cover, and cook until the meat is well caramelized, about 2 minutes.

4 Meanwhile, in a medium bowl, whisk together the extra-virgin olive oil and vinegar. Season the vinaigrette with salt and pepper. Add the tomato, onion, and mint and toss to combine.

5 Spoon the Greek yogurt onto a platter, top with the kebabs, and then top with tomato salad. Serve immediately.

½ cup **GREEK YOGURT**

3 tablespoons extra-virgin olive oil

Grated zest and juice of 2 **ORANGES**

2 **GARLIC** cloves, minced

1 tablespoon smoked paprika

1 tablespoon coriander seeds, toasted and ground

4 (4-ounce) boneless, skin-on **CHICKEN THIGHS**, pounded to a ¼-inch thickness and cut in thirds

Kosher salt and freshly ground black pepper

1 cup roughly chopped **FRESH CILANTRO** leaves

Like pork tenderloin, chicken is always on the lean side—even the dark meat. Using a yogurt marinade not only adds a nice tangy flavor to the chicken, but also helps to keep it from drying out. Before marinating the chicken, make sure you set aside half of the mixture to serve with the meal.

CHICKEN WITH SPICY YOGURT & CILANTRO

Makes 4 skewers; serves 4

1 Preheat a grill or grill pan to medium-high heat.

2 In a medium bowl, whisk together the yogurt, olive oil, orange zest and juice, garlic, paprika, and coriander. Set aside half of this dressing in a separate bowl to serve with the finished chicken. Season the chicken with salt and pepper and toss it in the remaining dressing. Thread 3 pieces of chicken onto each of 4 skewers.

3 Put the chicken skewers on the grill skin-side down, cover, and cook for 3 minutes. Flip the chicken, cover, and cook until the meat is well caramelized, about 2 minutes.

4 Remove the chicken from the grill, put on a platter, and garnish with the cilantro. Serve with the reserved yogurt sauce on the side.

This dish is a great example of "try it, you'll like it." I was never really a fan of fruit-based sauces on savory foods, but this recipe has become one of my favorite summertime grilling recipes. The tropical flavors go great with the shrimp, and they make this super simple recipe seem a little fancier. This glaze also works really well with chicken.

SHRIMP WITH PINEAPPLE GLAZE

Makes 8 skewers; serves 4

1 cup **PINEAPPLE JUICE**

¼ cup sherry vinegar

¼ cup packed light brown sugar

½ **JALAPEÑO** (split lengthwise)

1 **GARLIC** clove, smashed

1 tablespoon grated peeled **FRESH GINGER**

1 teaspoon coriander seeds, toasted and ground

1 teaspoon cumin seeds, toasted and ground

24 medium **SHRIMP** (about 1 pound) shelled and deveined

Kosher salt and freshly ground black pepper

¼ cup olive oil

1 Preheat a grill or grill pan to medium-high heat.

2 Put a nonreactive large saucepan over high heat and add the pineapple juice, vinegar, brown sugar, jalapeño, garlic, ginger, coriander, and cumin. Bring the mixture to a boil and allow to reduce until thickened while the shrimp is cooking, about 4 minutes.

3 Thread 3 shrimp onto each of 8 skewers, season with salt and pepper, and drizzle with the olive oil. Put the skewers on the grill, cover, and cook until the shrimp turn pink, about 2 minutes per side.

4 Remove the shrimp from the grill and put them on a platter. Strain the pineapple sauce into a bowl, brush it on both sides of the shrimp, and serve.

3

BETWEEN BREAD

LOOSE SAUSAGE & PEPPERS 77

SLOPPY MIKES 79

FRIED BOLOGNA & EGG 80

FRIED SALAMI WITH HOT PEPPERS 83

BREADED CHICKEN & MOZZARELLA WITH BASIL 84

PHILLY CHEESESTEAK WITH PROVOLONE 85

PORTOBELLO & ARUGULA WITH BLUE CHEESE 86

PATTY MELT 88

FLIP-STEAK & PEPPERS 89

PORK CUTLET WITH BROCCOLI RABE 90

SPICY 50/50 BURGER 93

BLUE COW BURGER 94

TOMATO TUNA MELT 95

TURKEY & AVOCADO MELT 96

ULTIMATE BLT 99

TUNA NIÇOISE SALAD SANDWICH 102

AS IS THE CASE with pasta, when it comes to sandwiches the possibilities are limitless. If you can stick it between two pieces of bread, you've got yourself a sandwich.

Of course, that doesn't mean that anything crammed between two pieces of wheat is automatically destined for the Sandwich Hall of Fame. The key to any great sandwich is a nice balance of flavors and textures and the proper bread-to-filling ratio.

For this chapter, I am assuming that—if you want to make a sandwich—you have some bread in your house. Call me crazy. So it's my pantry gimme for these recipes. And although I call for a specific type of bread in each recipe—be it a hoagie roll or French baguette—do not hesitate to swap out what you have on hand for what I call for. I would rather you try a recipe with what's in your bread basket than not at all. But do try and tailor the amount of filling to the bread type, as some bread is sturdier than others. I usually call for bread to be toasted, which not only adds a nice textural element but also makes the bun less likely to soak through and fall apart.

When it comes to sandwich pantry items I suggest you load up on as many condiments as you possibly can because they take your sandwich to the next level. I literally have a fridge full of at least a dozen different mustards and an equal number of hot sauces that I can reach for depending on my mood. And what good is a sandwich without a cold, crisp pickle? I always have a bunch of jars waiting to be opened or finished.

One of the best things about hitting The Feast celebration each summer in Cleveland's Little Italy neighborhood is digging into the amazing sausage and pepper sandwiches. Those sandwiches are built with sausage links, but for speed's sake, this one uses loose, bulk sausage. It may be quicker to prepare, but I promise it tastes just as good. Also, the classic is traditionally served in a hoagie roll. I prefer this version spooned onto a good old-fashioned roll.

LOOSE SAUSAGE & PEPPERS

Serves 4

3 tablespoons olive oil

1 pound SWEET ITALIAN SAUSAGE, removed from casings if not bulk

1 YELLOW ONION, thinly sliced (about 1 cup)

3 GARLIC cloves, minced

1 RED BELL PEPPER, thinly sliced

Kosher salt

4 Italian rolls, split and toasted

1 Put a large skillet over medium-high heat. Add the olive oil and then the sausage and cook, stirring with a wooden spoon to break up the meat, until browned, about 2 minutes. Scoot the sausage to one side of the pan. Add the onion, garlic, bell pepper, and a pinch of salt to the empty space and cook until the vegetables soften and begin to caramelize, about 2 minutes. Stir to combine the sausage and the vegetables and cook for 1 minute.

2 Spoon the sausage and pepper mixture onto the toasted hoagie rolls and serve.

Like most kids, I loved Sloppy Joe night at home. Unlike most kids, though, I never outgrew them! Sweet, zesty, and messy as heck, the sandwiches remain one of my favorite dishes. Sloppy Joes work great for a crowd, and it's one of the items I serve most often on football Sundays when I have company. The variations are almost endless, but this is the most requested version.

SLOPPY MIKES

Serves 6

2 tablespoons olive oil

1 pound **SPICY ITALIAN SAUSAGE**, removed from casings if not bulk

1 small **RED ONION**, minced

4 **GARLIC** cloves, minced

Kosher salt and freshly ground black pepper

1 (28-ounce) can crushed San Marzano tomatoes with juices

3 tablespoons packed light brown sugar

½ cup chopped **FRESH FLAT-LEAF PARSLEY** leaves

6 hamburger buns, split and toasted

1 Put a large skillet over medium-high heat. Add the olive oil and then the sausage and cook, stirring with a wooden spoon to break up the meat, until browned, about 2 minutes. Scoot the sausage to one side of the pan. Add the onion, garlic, and a pinch of salt to the empty space and cook, stirring occasionally, for 30 seconds. Taste and adjust the seasoning, adding salt and pepper as needed.

2 Add the tomatoes with their juices and the brown sugar and simmer for 2 minutes.

3 Remove from the heat and stir in the parsley. Spoon onto the toasted buns and serve.

3 tablespoons olive oil

4 (¾-inch-thick) slices **BOLOGNA**

4 **LARGE EGGS**

Kosher salt and freshly ground black pepper

4 tablespoons **MAYONNAISE**

8 slices sandwich bread

4 (⅛-inch-thick) slices **RED ONION**

1 Put 2 large sauté pans over medium heat. To the first one, add 1 tablespoon of the olive oil and then the bologna. Cook until the bologna is golden brown on both sides and starts to crisp, about 2 minutes per side.

2 Meanwhile, to the other pan, add the remaining 2 tablespoons olive oil and then the eggs. Season the eggs with salt and pepper. Cook until the whites are completely set but the yolks are still runny, about 2 minutes.

3 Spread 1 tablespoon of mayo on half of the slices of bread. Top each with a slice of bologna, a fried egg, and a slice of onion. Top with another slice of bread and serve.

In Ohio, we *looove* our fried bologna. In fact, when Mario Batali came to Cleveland and ate at B Spot for the first time, it was this fried bologna sandwich—not the burgers—that he couldn't (*and still won't*) stop talking about. Don't be afraid to cut the bologna on the thick side and give it a nice sear in the pan, which gives it a little snap. The soft-cooked egg ties it all together.

FRIED BOLOGNA & EGG

Serves 4

On weekends when I was growing up, my father would become Mr. Sandwich, whipping up all sorts of (mostly) delicious concoctions. This is one of his triumphs—a perfectly balanced handful of zesty salami, sweet basil, and melty cheese. Make sure to allow the salami to really crisp up in the pan; that is where all the flavor and texture come from.

FRIED SALAMI WITH HOT PEPPERS

Serves 4

1 pound thinly sliced SALAMI

2 RED BELL PEPPERS, thinly sliced

1 JALAPEÑO, sliced into thin rings

Kosher salt

4 slices PROVOLONE cheese

½ cup torn FRESH BASIL leaves

4 Kaiser rolls, split and toasted

1 Put a large skillet over medium-high heat. Working in batches so as not to crowd the pan, add the salami slices and cook until crisp, about 1 minute per side. As the slices are done, remove them to a plate.

2 When all the salami is out of the pan, add the bell and jalapeño peppers along with a good pinch of salt and cook until tender, about 2 minutes. Remove the peppers to a plate.

3 Reduce the heat under the pan to medium-low. Divide the salami into 4 equal piles, placing all of the piles in the pan. Top each pile with one-fourth of the bell and jalapeño peppers covered by 1 slice of cheese. Add 2 tablespoons water to the pan, cover with a lid, and allow the cheese to melt for 30 seconds.

4 Remove the lid and sprinkle each pile with one-fourth of the basil. Pile into the rolls and serve.

This recipe combines two great things in one: chicken Parmesan and sandwiches! Of course, I use the flavorful (and affordable) chicken thighs in place of bland breasts. The dark meat stays juicy and gives these sandwiches a more satisfying richness than the white-meat version.

BREADED CHICKEN & MOZZARELLA WITH BASIL

Serves 4

½ cup all-purpose flour

Kosher salt and freshly ground black pepper

3 LARGE EGGS

2 cups plain dry bread crumbs

2 cups freshly grated PARMESAN cheese

4 (4-ounce) boneless, skin-on CHICKEN THIGHS, pounded to a ¼-inch thickness

½ cup olive oil

½ pound FRESH MOZZARELLA cheese, cut into ¼-inch-thick slices

4 hoagie rolls, split and toasted

½ cup torn FRESH BASIL leaves

1 Put the flour in a shallow bowl and season well with salt and pepper. Put the eggs in another shallow bowl and beat them lightly. In a third shallow bowl, combine the bread crumbs and Parmesan and season well with salt and pepper.

2 Put a large skillet over medium-high heat.

3 Season both sides of the chicken with salt and pepper. Dredge each piece of chicken in the flour, coating both sides well. Shake off the excess. Dip the chicken into the beaten eggs, allowing the excess to drip off. Finally, coat the chicken in the bread crumbs.

4 Pour the oil into the pan. Add all 4 pieces of chicken skin-side down and cook until golden brown, about 2 minutes. Flip and cook until the other side is browned and the chicken is almost cooked through, about 2 minutes. Top each piece of chicken with mozzarella, cover, and cook until the cheese is melted, about 1 minute.

5 Put the chicken onto the buns, top with fresh basil, and serve.

While bread substitutions are fine in most sandwich recipes, for this classic sammie, you gotta go with a hoagie roll (preferably one from the famous Amoroso's bakery in Philly). If you can't source an authentic roll, look for one that is a little crusty on the outside, soft on the inside, and strong enough to support a load of meat, cheese, and veggies! I do this one with provolone, but when I'm in Philly, I always order it *"whiz wit"* (Cheez Whiz with onions).

PHILLY CHEESESTEAK WITH PROVOLONE

Serves 4

1 pound shaved **RIB EYE**

Kosher salt and freshly ground black pepper

4 tablespoons olive oil

2 cups thinly sliced **ONIONS** (from 1 large yellow)

2 cups thinly sliced **BUTTON MUSHROOMS** (from 8 ounces)

4 slices **PROVOLONE** cheese

4 hoagie rolls, split and toasted

1 Put a large skillet over high heat.

2 Season the rib eye slices on both sides with salt and pepper. Add 3 tablespoons of the olive oil to the preheated pan and then add the beef. Cook until the meat browns and the edges begin to curl, about 30 seconds. Flip the beef and cook until the meat is fully cooked, another 30 seconds. Remove the beef to a plate.

3 Reduce the heat to medium-high underneath the same skillet and add the remaining 1 tablespoon olive oil and then the onions, mushrooms, and a pinch of salt. Cook until the vegetables soften and begin to caramelize, about 3 minutes.

4 Arrange the vegetables in the skillet into 4 equal piles. Divide the rib eye into 4 equal portions and place one onto each pile of vegetables. Top each pile with a slice of provolone cheese. Reduce the heat to low, add 2 tablespoons water to the pan, cover the pan, and cook until the cheese is fully melted, about 30 seconds.

5 Pack one pile of veggies, meat, and cheese onto each hoagie roll and serve.

4 large **PORTOBELLO MUSHROOMS**

1 medium **RED ONION**, cut into ¼-inch-thick slices

¼ cup extra-virgin olive oil

¼ cup balsamic vinegar

Kosher salt and freshly ground black pepper

4 ounces **BUTTERMILK BLUE CHEESE**, crumbled (½ cup)

4 Kaiser rolls, split and toasted

2 cups loosely packed **ARUGULA**

1 Preheat a grill or grill pan to medium-high heat.

2 To clean the portobellos, remove the stems and scrape out the gills using a spoon. Drizzle the mushrooms and onion with the olive oil and vinegar and season liberally with salt and pepper.

3 Put the mushrooms and onions on the grill, close the lid (or cover, if using a grill pan), and cook until the mushrooms soften and the onions begin to char, about 3 minutes. Uncover, flip the mushrooms and onions, and cook uncovered for 1 minute. Top each mushroom with 1 ounce blue cheese. Cook uncovered until the cheese begins to melt, about 1 minute.

4 Put a mushroom onto each roll, top with 1 onion slice and ½ cup arugula, and serve.

B Spot is a carnivore's paradise, with meaty burgers, brats, and bologna sandwiches. But we do have something for the veg heads: a portobello, onion, and arugula sandwich just like this one. Of course, we call it the Why? Burger and offer to top it with bacon for no additional charge. Why? Because everything is better with bacon!

PORTOBELLO & ARUGULA WITH BLUE CHEESE

Serves 4

1 pound **GROUND BEEF** (80% lean)

Kosher salt and freshly ground black pepper

3 tablespoons olive oil

1 small **YELLOW ONION**, thinly sliced

3 tablespoons **UNSALTED BUTTER**

8 slices rye bread

8 tablespoons **MAYONNAISE**

4 slices **SWISS CHEESE**

What happens when you cross a hamburger with a grilled cheese sandwich? You end up with a patty melt, one of the most delicious foods imaginable. This diner classic combines the meaty goodness of a burger with the buttery crunch of grilled cheese. Sautéed onions add some sweetness while the rye gives it a touch of nuttiness.

PATTY MELT

Serves 4

1 Put a large skillet over medium-high heat and a second large skillet over medium heat.

2 Form the meat into 4 patties, each about ½ inch thick. Season the patties on both sides with salt and pepper. To the first pan, add the olive oil and then the patties, arranging them on one side of the pan. Add the onion to the open space and season with salt and pepper. Cook the burgers without moving until a good crust forms, about 2 minutes. Flip the burgers and cook until heavily caramelized and medium-rare, about 2 minutes. Occasionally stir the onions.

3 Meanwhile, add 2 tablespoons of the butter to the second pan. When the butter is melted, add 4 slices of the bread to the pan to toast. Spread 2 tablespoons mayonnaise on each of the remaining 4 slices of bread.

4 Put a burger on top of each slice of rye bread in the skillet. Top each burger with one-fourth of the sautéed onions, 1 slice cheese, and the other slice of bread, mayonnaise-side down. Add the remaining 1 tablespoon butter to the pan, flip the sandwiches, and cook until golden brown and the cheese has melted, about 1 minute.

5 Remove the sandwiches to a cutting board, slice in half, and serve.

1 pound shaved RIB EYE

Kosher salt and freshly ground black pepper

3 tablespoons olive oil

2 cups thinly sliced ONION

1 JALAPEÑO, thinly sliced into rings, with seeds

2 cups thinly sliced RED BELL PEPPER (from 2)

4 slices GRUYÈRE cheese (Swiss will also work)

4 hoagie rolls, split and toasted

This is a tasty twist on the classic Philly. I use the same delicious shaved rib eye, but I spice it up a bit with jalapeño, add sweet bell peppers, and use the more flavorful Gruyère cheese. It might not be authentic, but it still tastes like heaven.

FLIP-STEAK & PEPPERS

Serves 4

1 Put a large skillet over high heat.

2 Season the rib eye slices on both sides with salt and pepper. Add 2 tablespoons of the oil to the preheated pan and then add the beef. Cook until the meat browns and the edges begin to curl, about 30 seconds. Flip the beef and cook until the meat is fully cooked, another 30 seconds. Remove the beef to a plate.

3 Reduce the heat to medium-high underneath the same skillet and add the remaining 1 tablespoon oil and then the onion, jalapeño, bell peppers, and a pinch of salt. Cook until the vegetables soften and begin to caramelize, about 3 minutes.

4 Arrange the vegetables in the skillet into 4 equal piles. Divide the rib eye into 4 equal portions and place one onto each pile of vegetables. Top each pile with a slice of Gruyère. Reduce the heat to low, add 2 tablespoons water to the pan, cover the pan, and cook until the cheese is fully melted, about 30 seconds.

5 Pack one pile of veggies, meat, and cheese onto each hoagie roll and serve.

When I have all kinds of time on my hands, I love to roast a huge porchetta and make sandwiches loaded with the flavors of an authentic Philly roast pork sandwich. Of course, that doesn't happen every day, so I make this quick version instead. If you close your eyes and take a bite, you can imagine being in the Reading Terminal Market.

PORK CUTLET WITH BROCCOLI RABE

Serves 4

½ cup all-purpose flour

Kosher salt and freshly ground black pepper

2 **LARGE EGGS**, beaten

1 cup plain dry bread crumbs

8 (2-ounce) pieces of **PORK LOIN**, pounded to a ¼-inch thickness

5 tablespoons olive oil

2 cups (1-inch pieces) **BROCCOLI RABE**

3 **GARLIC** cloves, sliced

1 teaspoon crushed red pepper flakes

4 sourdough rolls, split and toasted

½ cup freshly grated **PARMESAN** cheese

1 Put the flour in a shallow bowl and season well with salt and black pepper. Put the eggs in another shallow bowl and beat them lightly. To a third shallow bowl, combine the bread crumbs and Parmesan and season well with salt and black pepper.

2 Put 2 large skillets over medium-high heat.

3 Season both sides of the pork with salt and black pepper. Working with one piece of meat at a time, dredge the pork in the flour, making sure to coat both sides well. Shake off the excess. Dip the pork into the beaten eggs, allowing the excess to drip off. Finally, lay the pork in the bread crumbs, turning and pressing to fully coat both sides.

4 Add 3 tablespoons of the olive oil to one of the preheated pans. Arrange all 8 pieces of pork in the pan and cook until golden brown, about 2 minutes per side.

5 Meanwhile, heat the remaining 2 tablespoons olive oil in the second pan. Add the broccoli rabe and a good pinch of salt and cook for 2 minutes. Add the garlic and red pepper flakes and cook until the broccoli rabe is tender, about 2 minutes.

6 Put 2 pork cutlets onto each roll bottom, top with broccoli rabe, sprinkle with Parmesan, and top with the other half of the roll and serve.

For those of you who refuse to eat your burgers anything shy of burnt, this recipe is for you! By making the patties with 50 percent beef and 50 percent sausage—hence "50/50 Burger"—they stay juicy even at well-done, thanks to the extra fat from the sausage. This recipe calls for zesty chorizo, but the technique works just as well with Italian sausage.

SPICY 50/50 BURGER

Serves 4

¾ pound GROUND BEEF (80% lean)

¾ pound FRESH CHORIZO, removed from casings if not bulk

Kosher salt and freshly ground black pepper

2 tablespoons extra-virgin olive oil

4 slices MONTEREY JACK cheese

4 challah-style buns, split and toasted

1 cup FRESH CILANTRO leaves

1 Put a large skillet over medium-high heat.

2 In a bowl, mix to combine the ground beef and chorizo. Form the meat into 4 patties, each about ¾ inch thick. Season the patties on both sides with salt and pepper.

3 Add the olive oil to the preheated pan, then add the patties and, with a spatula, press each to form thin burgers. Cook without moving until a good crust forms, about 2 minutes. Flip the burgers and cook until heavily caramelized, about 2 minutes. Reduce the heat to medium-low and top each burger with a slice of cheese. Add 2 tablespoons water to the pan, cover, and allow the cheese to melt for 1 minute.

4 Put 1 burger onto each bun bottom, top with ¼ cup cilantro and the other half of the bun, and serve.

1 pound **GROUND BEEF** (80% lean)

Kosher salt and freshly ground black pepper

¼ cup crumbled **BLUE CHEESE**

4 hamburger buns, split and toasted

1 small **RED ONION**, sliced into four thin rings

1 cup **ARUGULA**

"Blue Cow" is just a funny way of saying hamburger with blue cheese—but the taste is no joke. Blue cheese packs so much more flavor than other cheeses, elevating this burger to new heights. Raw red onion and perky arugula help punch through the richness of the meat and cheese.

BLUE COW BURGER

Serves 4

1 Preheat a grill or grill pan to medium-high heat.

2 Form the meat into 4 patties, each ½ inch thick. Season the patties on both sides with salt and pepper. Put the patties on the grill and cook without moving for 3 minutes. Flip, top each burger with 1 tablespoon of the blue cheese, and cook until medium-rare and the cheese begins to melt, about 2 minutes. Remove the burgers from the grill.

3 Put 1 burger onto each bun bottom, top with a slice of red onion, ¼ cup arugula, and the other half of the bun, and serve.

2 (7-ounce) jars **OLIVE OIL–PACKED TUNA** (Tonnino is my favorite)

⅓ cup mayonnaise

1 tablespoon Dijon mustard

1 tablespoon red wine vinegar

2 tablespoons capers, rinsed, drained, and finely chopped

¼ cup thinly sliced **SCALLIONS**, green and white parts

2 tablespoons finely chopped **FRESH FLAT-LEAF PARSLEY** leaves

¼ teaspoon celery seed

Kosher salt and freshly ground black pepper

1 large **TOMATO**, cut into into 6 (½-inch-thick) slices

6 slices **SWISS CHEESE**

For those of you who suffer from gluten intolerance—or are just trying to cut back on carbs—but still crave sandwiches, this one's for you. It's an open-face tuna sandwich that is meaty, satisfying, delicious, *and* bread-free. Look for a really large tomato or use two slightly smaller ones, as you want the slices to be good and thick.

TOMATO TUNA MELT

Serves 6

1 Preheat the oven to 350°F.

2 In a large bowl, mix together the tuna and the oil it's packed in, the mayonnaise, mustard, vinegar, capers, scallions, parsley, and celery seed. Season with salt and pepper.

3 Arrange the tomato slices on a baking sheet and top each one with one-sixth of the tuna salad. Top each pile with a slice of Swiss cheese. Place in the oven to cook until the cheese is fully melted, about 4 minutes. Serve immediately.

I love a good melt—they're like souped-up grilled cheese sandwiches. And like grilled cheeses they are crisp and toasty, warm and melty, and just the right kind of messy. I like the way avocado adds another dimension of richness to the party. And in a small way, it makes me feel like I'm eating healthy.

TURKEY & AVOCADO MELT

Serves 4

6 tablespoons Dijon mustard

8 slices of your favorite bread

1 **AVOCADO**, thinly sliced

Kosher salt and freshly ground black pepper

1 pound thinly sliced **SMOKED TURKEY BREAST**

4 slices **GRUYÈRE** cheese (Swiss will also work)

4 tablespoons **MAYONNAISE**

2 tablespoons olive oil

1 Put a large skillet over medium heat.

2 Spread the mustard onto all of the slices of bread. Season the avocado slices with salt and pepper. Build each sandwich on half the bread, using one-fourth of the turkey, one-fourth of the avocado slices, and 1 slice of cheese. Top the sandwiches with the other slices of bread, mustard-side down. Spread 1 tablespoon mayonnaise onto the top and bottom of each sandwich.

3 To the preheated pan, add the olive oil and then the sandwiches. Cook until golden brown, about 2 minutes. Flip the sandwiches and cook until golden on the second side, about 2 minutes.

4 Remove the sandwiches to a cutting board, slice in half, and serve.

Question: What's better than a BLT?
Answer: Nothing!

Talk about a match made in heaven. Something magical happens when salty, smoky bacon collides with juicy, ripe tomatoes. At home, I make a million different variations of the basic bacon, lettuce, and tomato sandwich. But this one—with the addition of creamy avocado and zippy Dijon mustard—is one of my all-time favorites.

ULTIMATE BLT

Serves 4

1 pound sliced **SMOKY BACON**

4 tablespoons Dijon mustard

2 tablespoons hot sauce

4 brioche-style buns, split and toasted

1 **AVOCADO**, sliced

Kosher salt and freshly ground black pepper

1 large **TOMATO**, preferably heirloom, cut into 4 thick slices

½ cup torn **FRESH BASIL** leaves

1 Put a large skillet over medium-high heat. Add the bacon and cook, flipping once, until crisp, about 2 minutes per side. Remove to a paper towel–lined plate.

2 Meanwhile, in a small bowl, whisk together the mustard and hot sauce. Spread the mustard mixture onto each bun. Season the avocado slices with salt and pepper.

3 Build each sandwich by topping the bun bottom with 1 slice of tomato, one-fourth of the avocado slices, a few strips of bacon, and 2 tablespoons basil. Top with the other half of the bun and serve with an ice-cold beer!

2 (7-ounce) jars OLIVE OIL–PACKED TUNA

½ cup chopped OLIVE OIL–PACKED
SUNDRIED TOMATOES, plus 2 tablespoons
of the oil

2 hard-boiled LARGE EGGS, chopped

½ cup chopped KALAMATA OLIVES

¼ cup chopped FRESH FLAT-LEAF PARSLEY
leaves

3 tablespoons Dijon mustard

Pinch of crushed red pepper flakes

Kosher salt and freshly ground black pepper

1 French baguette, halved lengthwise and toasted

This is a sandwich version of the classic *salade Niçoise*, a French salad that features hard-boiled eggs, olives, and good-quality jarred tuna. For the best results, use really good tuna (Tonnino is my favorite brand) and great bread.

TUNA NIÇOISE SALAD SANDWICH

Serves 4

1 In a large bowl, mix to combine the tuna and the oil it's packed in, the sundried tomatoes and their oil, the eggs, olives, parsley, mustard, and red pepper flakes. Season the salad with salt and black pepper.

2 Spread the salad onto the bottom half of the baguette. Top with the other half of the bread, slice into four equal portions, and serve.

4

PACKET PERFECTION

WHATEVER YOU CALL IT—
cooking in parchment, *en papillote,* or *al cartoccio*—cooking in packets is a woefully underutilized method.

Traditionally, this cooking technique involves cooking foods in parchment paper, which puffs up and turns golden brown in the oven. While parchment certainly is impressive, good old aluminum foil works just as well. Regardless of the wrapper, the result is moist, tender, and flavorful food.

This chapter is filled with great recipes, and I hope they'll inspire some creativity in you when it comes to pouch cooking. Don't be afraid to mix and match and experiment. In addition to requiring no pots or pans—a huge bonus!—cooking in packets makes it easy to customize individual portions. If somebody in your family doesn't like dill, for example, you can easily omit it or substitute parsley. Meats and veggies, too, can be swapped in and out with ease.

I like to serve the packets unopened on a plate so that when diners bust into them, they are greeted by a warm puff of fragrant air. To speed things up in the cooking process, make sure all the ingredients are at room temperature when they go into the pouch and onto the grill.

2 pounds **KIELBASA**, sliced on the bias

2 cups **SAUERKRAUT**

½ cup thinly sliced **RED ONION**

½ cup roughly chopped **FRESH FLAT-LEAF PARSLEY** leaves

1 tablespoon caraway seeds

Kosher salt and freshly ground black pepper

1 (12-ounce) bottle **IPA-STYLE BEER**

1 Preheat a grill or grill pan to medium-high heat.

2 Lay out 4 large pieces of aluminum foil. In the center of each piece, put one-fourth of the kielbasa, ½ cup sauerkraut, one-fourth of the red onion, and 2 tablespoons parsley. Season each pile with the caraway seeds and salt and pepper. Bring up all 4 corners of the foil to begin to form a pouch. Before sealing, split the beer equally among the packets. Tightly seal each packet.

3 Put the packets on the grill and close the lid (or cover, if using a grill pan). Cook until hot throughout, about 4 minutes. Remove from the grill, open, and serve immediately.

To me, this is a little bundle of Cleveland. When I open up the foil package, the aroma immediately takes me back to the West Side Market and all those smoked sausage sandwiches I would eat with my grandfather. While this isn't a sandwich, if you pair it with some grilled bread and dark mustard, you'll have all the same elements.

KIELBASA & 'KRAUT

Serves 4

Mussels with white wine and garlic is such a classic dish. But why bother having to clean a pan when you can do the whole thing in foil? This dish works just as well with small clams, but you'll have to double the liquid and the cook time. Use up any squishy, over-ripe tomatoes here because they break down quickly into the sauce. You're going to want some crusty bread with this one to mop up the flavorful cooking juices.

MUSSELS WITH WHITE WINE & GARLIC

Serves 4

2 pounds **MUSSELS**, cleaned

4 cups **CHERRY TOMATOES**

½ cup chopped **FRESH FLAT-LEAF PARSLEY** leaves

4 **GARLIC** cloves, minced

½ cup extra-virgin olive oil

1 tablespoon crushed red pepper flakes

Kosher salt and freshly ground black pepper

2 cups dry **WHITE WINE**

1 Preheat a grill or grill pan to medium-high heat.

2 Lay out 4 large pieces of aluminum foil. In the center of each piece, put one-fourth of the mussels, 1 cup tomatoes, 2 tablespoons parsley, one-fourth of the garlic, and 2 tablespoons olive oil. Season each pile with the red pepper flakes and salt and black pepper. Bring up all 4 corners of the foil to begin to form a pouch. Before sealing, add ½ cup white wine to each packet. Tightly seal each packet.

3 Put the packets on the grill and close the lid (or cover, if using a grill pan). Cook until the mussels open, about 4 minutes. Remove from the grill, open, and serve immediately.

1 pound shelled and deveined **LARGE SHRIMP**

½ pound dried or smoked **CHORIZO**, cut into ¼-inch-thick slices

4 tablespoons chopped **FRESH OREGANO** leaves

1 teaspoon cumin seeds, toasted and ground

1 (14.5-ounce) can diced San Marzano tomatoes with juices

Kosher salt and freshly ground black pepper

Grated zest and juice of 2 **ORANGES**

4 tablespoons extra-virgin olive oil

In my opinion, shrimp and spicy sausage are like peas and carrots—they always go together. You can definitely enjoy this meal as is. But to make it really special, serve it with some buttery grits or polenta. You'll have a great and filling meal for not a lot of time, hassle, or money.

SHRIMP & CHORIZO

Serves 4

1 Preheat a grill or grill pan to medium-high heat.

2 Lay out 4 large pieces of aluminum foil. In the center of each piece, put one-fourth of the shrimp, one-fourth of the chorizo, 1 tablespoon oregano, ¼ teaspoon cumin, and ½ cup tomatoes with juices. Bring up all 4 corners of the foil to begin to form a pouch. Before sealing, season each packet with salt and pepper and add one-fourth of the orange zest and juice, 2 tablespoons water, and 1 tablespoon olive oil. Tightly seal each packet.

3 Put the packets on the grill and close the lid (or cover, if using a grill pan). Cook until the shrimp are pink and cooked through, about 4 minutes. Remove from the grill, open, and serve immediately.

4 (6-ounce) skinless COD FILLETS

Kosher salt

4 tablespoons chopped FRESH DILL

2 GARLIC cloves, minced

Grated zest and juice of 2 LEMONS

8 tablespoons dry WHITE WINE

8 tablespoons extra-virgin olive oil

1 Preheat a grill or grill pan to medium-high heat.

2 Season the cod on both sides with salt. Lay out 4 large pieces of aluminum foil. In the center of each piece, put 1 piece of cod, 1 tablespoon dill, and one-fourth of the garlic. Bring up all 4 corners of the foil to begin to form a pouch. Before sealing, add one-fourth of the lemon zest and juice, 2 tablespoons white wine, and 2 tablespoons olive oil to each packet. Tightly seal each packet.

3 Put the packets on the grill and close the lid (or cover, if using a grill pan). Cook until hot throughout, about 4 minutes. Remove from the grill, open, and serve immediately.

This is Greece in a packet! Cod and lemon are such a simple, beautiful flavor combination, and the fresh dill really bumps up the brightness factor. Don't skimp on the extra-virgin olive oil here because it really adds to the overall quality of the dish. Also, this recipe works great with any flaky fish, so choose whatever looks the freshest.

COD WITH DILL & LEMON

Serves 4

Variations of this classic dish appear in countless *tavernas* throughout Greece. It is traditionally prepared in big earthenware pots cooked in wood-fired ovens. This version is a little easier to manage at home. When you pop in the feta at the last moment, it begins to melt into the sauce, giving it and the shrimp a salty richness.

SHRIMP WITH FETA & TOMATO

Serves 4

1½ pounds shelled and deveined **MEDIUM SHRIMP**

4 cups **CHERRY TOMATOES**

½ cup **FRESH DILL**

½ cup extra-virgin olive oil

Kosher salt and freshly ground black pepper

2 cups dry **WHITE WINE**

1 cup crumbled **FETA** cheese

1 Preheat a grill or grill pan to medium-high heat.

2 Lay out 4 large pieces of aluminum foil. In the center of each piece, put one-fourth of the shrimp, 1 cup tomatoes, 2 tablespoons dill, and 2 tablespoons olive oil. Season each pile with salt and pepper. Bring up all 4 corners of the foil to begin to form a pouch. Before sealing, add ½ cup wine to each packet. Tightly seal each packet.

3 Put the packets on the grill and close the lid (or cover, if using a grill pan). Cook until the shrimp are pink and cooked through, about 4 minutes. Remove from the grill, open, and top each pouch with ¼ cup feta. Serve immediately.

2 pounds **ANDOUILLE**, sliced on the bias

2 cups small-diced **ZUCCHINI**

1 cup toasted **ALMONDS**

1 cup chopped **FRESH CILANTRO** leaves

1 (14-ounce) can diced San Marzano tomatoes with juices

½ tablespoon cumin seeds, toasted and ground

Kosher salt and freshly ground black pepper

1 cup dry **WHITE WINE**

Andouille sausage is a delicious Southern staple, used in classic Cajun dishes like jambalaya and gumbo. It is spicy, smoky, and jam-packed with flavor. When you cook it, some of the wonderful spices like paprika and garlic seep out and flavor the foods around it—and everything picks up a nice smokiness. If you can't find andouille, you can substitute kielbasa or chorizo—just make sure the sausage is cured, not fresh.

ANDOUILLE WITH ZUCCHINI, ALMONDS & TOMATO

Serves 4

1 Preheat a grill or grill pan to medium-high heat.

2 Lay out 4 large pieces of aluminum foil. In the center of each piece, put one-fourth of the andouille, ½ cup zucchini, ¼ cup almonds, ¼ cup cilantro, and a little less than ½ cup tomatoes with juices. Season with the cumin and salt and pepper. Bring up all 4 corners of the foil to begin to form a pouch. Before sealing, add ¼ cup white wine to each packet. Tightly seal each packet.

3 Put the packets on the grill and close the lid (or cover, if using a grill pan). Cook until hot throughout, about 4 minutes. Remove from the grill, open, and serve immediately.

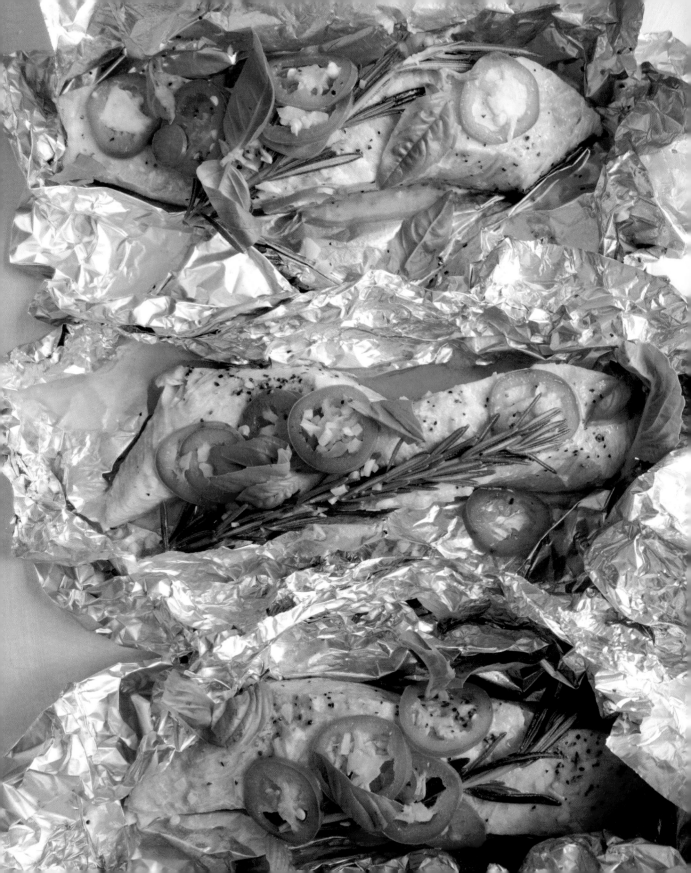

Thanks to its robust flavor, salmon is one of the few types of fish that can stand up to rosemary, an assertive herb that typically is paired with meat. Along those lines, this dish also can handle a good amount of heat, so I tend to go heavy with the red pepper flakes. Feel free to tone it down to accommodate your heat tolerance.

SALMON WITH ROSEMARY AND GARLIC

Serves 4

4 (6-ounce) skinless SALMON FILLETS

Kosher salt and freshly ground black pepper

4 sprigs FRESH ROSEMARY

1 tablespoon crushed red pepper flakes (or sliced red chile, if you have it)

½ cup extra-virgin olive oil

2 GARLIC cloves, minced

2 cups DRY WHITE WINE

1 cup torn FRESH BASIL leaves

1 Preheat a grill or grill pan to medium-high heat.

2 Season the salmon on both sides with salt and black pepper. Lay out 4 large pieces of aluminum foil. In the center of each piece, put 1 piece of salmon, 1 sprig rosemary, ¾ teaspoon red pepper flakes, and 2 tablespoons olive oil. Evenly distribute the garlic among the piles and season with salt and black pepper. Bring up all 4 corners of the foil to begin to form a pouch. Before sealing, add ½ cup white wine to each packet. Tightly seal the packets.

3 Put the packets on the grill and close the lid (or cover, if using a grill pan). Cook until hot throughout, about 4 minutes. Remove from the grill, open, and top each with ¼ cup basil. Serve immediately.

5

EGGSCELLENT

A HEN LAYS AN EGG almost every single day, which I think is proof that we are supposed to eat and enjoy them just as frequently!

I can't imagine a more versatile, affordable, and delicious food than eggs. It's no wonder that they call the egg Nature's Perfect Food.

I know we usually think of eggs as a breakfast staple, but they work just as well for lunch, brunch, dinner, or a midnight snack. And when it comes to quick and easy, eggs are pretty tough to top.

As with cooking meats, it's best to not overcook eggs or they will get dry and unappetizing. You want to retain their silky, creamy, luxurious qualities. But as far as add-ons and mix-ins, the sky's the limit because eggs work well with almost any meat, cheese, or vegetable.

It has never been easier to find farm-fresh eggs from pastured chickens, and believe me, using them makes a big difference in flavor. Most farmers' markets carry them, and they aren't much more expensive per egg than the grocery store ones, which often come from inhumane factory farms. If you do buy your eggs from the grocery store, look for organic, free-range ones, which are better than the so-called "cage-free" ones.

Salami and eggs is a classic deli dish where you brown the meat a little, add the eggs, and scramble them all together. It is pretty tough to improve on the original, but the addition of melty, bold Fontina cheese and fresh basil is a good start. Also, this recipe is a frittata, which is a tad more elegant than a plate of scrambled eggs.

FRIED SALAMI & FONTINA FRITTATA

Serves 6

2 tablespoons olive oil

4 ounces thinly sliced SALAMI, cut into strips

8 LARGE EGGS

¼ cup HEAVY CREAM

Kosher salt and freshly ground black pepper

1 cup grated FONTINA cheese

½ cup torn FRESH BASIL leaves

1 Preheat the broiler to medium-high.

2 Put a large ovenproof nonstick skillet over medium-high heat. Add the olive oil and then the salami. Cook, stirring occasionally, until crisp, about 2 minutes.

3 Meanwhile, in a medium bowl, whisk together the eggs and cream. Season with salt and pepper. Add the eggs to the salami and cook, stirring gently from time to time, until the eggs begin to set up but are still a little runny, about 2 minutes. Top with the Fontina and put under the broiler until golden brown, about 1 minute.

4 Slide the frittata out of the pan onto a cutting board. Top with the basil, then slice and serve.

This flavorful frittata is a play off *spanakopita*, the amazing Greek dish with phyllo, spinach, and feta. Feta and spinach make such a classic pairing because the salty cheese goes great with the mineral qualities of the spinach. Don't wait for the feta to melt too much—it isn't really a "melting" cheese—though it will start to wilt a bit.

FETA & SPINACH FRITTATA

Serves 6

2 tablespoons UNSALTED BUTTER

4 cups packed BABY SPINACH

Kosher salt and freshly ground black pepper

8 LARGE EGGS

¼ cup HEAVY CREAM

½ cup crumbled FETA cheese

1 Preheat the broiler to high.

2 Put a large ovenproof nonstick skillet over medium-high heat. Add the butter and then the spinach along with a pinch of salt. Cook, stirring as needed, until the spinach is wilted, about 1 minute.

3 In a medium bowl, whisk together the eggs and cream. Season with salt and pepper. Add the eggs to the spinach and cook, stirring gently from time to time, until the eggs begin to set up but are still a little runny, about 2 minutes. Top with the feta and put under the broiler until the cheese begins to melt, about 1 minute.

4 Slide the frittata out of the pan onto a cutting board. Slice and serve.

2 tablespoons olive oil

1 **SHALLOT**, minced

1 **GARLIC** clove, minced

1 **JALAPEÑO**, cut into thin rings

Kosher salt and freshly ground black pepper

1 (28-ounce) can diced San Marzano tomatoes with juices

¼ cup chopped **FRESH FLAT-LEAF PARSLEY** leaves

8 **LARGE EGGS**

This recipe was inspired by my cohost Chef Mario Batali. Poaching eggs in a spicy tomato sauce cooks and flavors the eggs at the same time. I would serve these eggs on a piece of good toast or an English muffin and top the whole thing with the spicy sauce.

EGGS IN HELL

Serves 4

1 Put a large Dutch oven over medium heat. Add the olive oil, shallot, garlic, jalapeño, and a pinch of salt and cook for 1 minute. Add the tomatoes with juices and allow the sauce to come up to a simmer. Season with salt and pepper and then stir in the parsley.

2 Carefully crack the eggs into the sauce so as not to pop the yolks, leaving a little space between each egg. Reduce the heat to medium-low, cover, and cook until the whites are set and the yolks are still runny, about 2 minutes.

3 Scoop out the eggs and transfer to plates. Top with sauce and serve.

2 tablespoons olive oil

1 cup halved **CHERRY TOMATOES**

Kosher salt and freshly ground black pepper

8 **LARGE EGGS**

¼ cup **HEAVY CREAM**

½ cup freshly grated **PARMESAN** cheese

2 ounces thinly sliced **PROSCIUTTO**

1 Preheat the broiler to high.

2 Put a large ovenproof nonstick skillet over medium-high heat. Add the olive oil and tomatoes along with a pinch of salt. Cook until the tomatoes soften and begin to release their juices, about 1 minute.

3 In a medium bowl, whisk together the eggs and cream. Season with salt and pepper. Add the eggs to the tomatoes and cook, stirring gently from time to time, until the eggs begin to set up but are still a little runny, about 2 minutes. Top with the Parmesan and put under the broiler until slightly golden, about 1 minute.

4 Slide the frittata out of the pan onto a cutting board. Top with the prosciutto, then slice and serve.

Prosciutto and Parmesan both come from the Parma region of Italy, making them perfect partners in the food world. In this recipe, you don't cook the prosciutto, but instead top the still-warm frittata with thin slices of the salty ham, which soften and begin to "melt" into the eggs.

PROSCIUTTO & TOMATO FRITTATA

Serves 6

Kosher salt and freshly ground black pepper

¼ cup white wine vinegar

1 cup freshly grated PARMESAN cheese

¼ cup chopped FRESH FLAT-LEAF PARSLEY leaves

1 GARLIC clove, minced

1 large TOMATO, cut into 8 slices

8 LARGE EGGS

For some reason, poaching eggs scares some people. Probably because when they've tried to do it, they ended up with loose and wispy eggs instead of nice, tight bundles. There are a couple tricks to doing it right. First, adding vinegar to the water helps the eggs to set more quickly. And second, swirling the water and lowering each egg into the middle of the vortex helps keep them together until they set up.

POACHED EGGS PARMESAN

Serves 4

1 Preheat the broiler to medium-high.

2 To poach the eggs, put a medium saucepan over medium-high heat. Add 6 cups water, 1 tablespoon salt, and the vinegar. Bring to a simmer.

3 In a small bowl, mix together the Parmesan, parsley, and garlic. Season the sliced tomatoes with salt and pepper and put them in a large ovenproof skillet. Top the tomato slices with the Parmesan mixture and put the pan under the broiler until the cheese begins to brown, about 2 minutes.

4 Meanwhile, crack each egg into its own little bowl. Reduce the heat under the poaching liquid to medium-low. With a spoon, create a large (but gentle) whirlpool in the water by stirring in one direction around the perimeter of the pan. Then gently lower each egg into the center of the pan. Poach untouched until the eggs are set enough to be lifted out of the water without breaking but the yolks are still runny, about 3 minutes.

5 Put 2 slices of tomato onto each plate. Top each tomato with 1 egg. Season each egg with salt and pepper and serve.

This dish is a twist on something called a one-eyed jack (or toad-in-the-hole, depending on where you're from), which is a piece of bread with a hole cut out of the middle to cradle an egg. Here, I swap the bread for slices of rich and creamy avocado. If you've never tasted a crispy sautéed avocado, you are in for a real treat.

EGGS IN AVOCADO WITH TOMATO & BASIL

Serves 4

2 **AVOCADOS**

Kosher salt and freshly ground black pepper

4 tablespoons olive oil

4 **LARGE EGGS**

1 cup halved **CHERRY TOMATOES**

½ cup torn **FRESH BASIL** leaves

Grated zest and juice of 1 **LIME**

1 Put a large Dutch oven over medium-high heat.

2 Halve each avocado lengthwise. Peel and pit the halves. Using a spoon, scoop out some of the avocado where the pits were to form a donut hole that goes clear through each half. Lay the avocados out on a cutting board, top with plastic wrap, and gently press down to slightly flatten the pieces. The idea is to make thick but flat slices, each with a hole in the center. Season both sides with salt and pepper.

3 To the preheated pan, add 2 tablespoons of the olive oil. Add the avocado slices cut-side down and cook until they begin to brown, about 1 minute. Flip the avocados and carefully crack 1 egg into each hole. Season the eggs with salt and pepper. Reduce the heat to medium-low, cover, and cook until the egg whites have set up but the yolks are still runny, about 3 minutes.

4 Meanwhile, in a medium bowl, mix together the tomatoes, basil, lime zest and juice, and remaining 2 tablespoons olive oil. Season with salt and pepper.

5 Top each avocado and egg with some tomato salad and serve.

CHICKEN PAILLARD SALAD 135

BREADED PORK LOIN WITH APPLE SALAD 136

TURKEY CUTLET WITH BRUSSELS SPROUT SALAD 139

CHICKEN LIVERS WITH ARUGULA & BACON 140

BREADED CHICKEN BREAST WITH TOMATOES & BASIL 142

MINUTE STEAK WITH FRIED EGG & WARM ARUGULA SALAD 145

CHICKEN THIGHS IN TOMATO & OLIVE SAUCE 146

6

MAN WITH A PAN

BREADED BEEF CUTLET WITH SPINACH & MUSHROOM SALAD 148

CHICKEN AMANDINE 150

SHRIMP WITH ORANGE & PINE NUTS 151

TROUT & GREEN BEANS 153

CHICKEN MARSALA 154

PORK SALTIMBOCCA 157

SALISBURY STEAK 158

GARLIC CHICKEN WITH ASPARAGUS 160

PORK CUTLET WITH PEACHES & ALMONDS 163

TURKEY CUTLET WITH LEMON, CAPERS & BROWN BUTTER 164

CHICKEN MILANESE 165

CHICKEN DIABLO 166

PORK SCHNITZEL 168

CHICKEN WITH SNOW PEAS & RED PEPPER FLAKES 171

SWISS STEAK 172

BEEF TRI-TIP WITH SPICY PEPPERS 174

PORK & BROCCOLI STIR-FRY 177

BEEF TRI-TIP WITH MUSHROOM SAUCE 178

CHICKEN WITH BROWN BUTTER & ORANGE 179

THIS IS AS CLOSE to restaurant-style cooking as you'll get in this cookbook. Things move fast thanks to high heat, pan sauces, and some multitasking.

Make sure you read through the entire recipe before starting so you know what is coming next. Take your meat or fish out of the fridge ahead of time to allow it to come to room temperature. Have all your ingredients prepped and ready to go. Many of these recipes involve breading with a flour, egg, and bread crumb process. This can be done ahead of time. Make sure your pans are good and hot. You can certainly cook over medium heat if that makes you more comfortable, but the recipes will take a little longer to finish.

Just because things move fast in these recipes doesn't mean you can rush certain steps. After putting meat or fish in a pan, allow it to cook untouched until it develops a slight crust and releases from the pan, 2 to 3 minutes. Not only does this prevent the meat from sticking to the pan and falling apart, the browning process is where a lot of the flavor comes from.

Finally, don't forget to taste and season dressings, vinaigrettes, and pan sauces. There is nothing worse than underseasoned food!

This is a classic French bistro salad. But despite being a French restaurant staple, it is quick and easy to prepare at home. Frisée is a frizzy, curly lettuce that has great crunch and a slight bitterness, which adds a nice contrast to buttery sautéed chicken. This is the kind of salad you can eat every day and not feel guilty. (Of course, I leave the skin on the chicken breast, but the choice is yours.)

CHICKEN PAILLARD SALAD

Serves 4

¼ cup olive oil

4 (6-ounce) boneless, skin-on CHICKEN BREAST halves, pounded to a ¼-inch thickness

Kosher salt and freshly ground black pepper

2 tablespoons red wine vinegar

2 tablespoons Dijon mustard

¼ cup extra-virgin olive oil

½ cup chopped FRESH TARRAGON leaves

4 cups FRISÉE, cut into bite-size pieces

½ cup thinly sliced RED ONION

1 Put a large skillet over medium-high heat.

2 Add the olive oil to the hot pan. Season both sides of the chicken with salt and pepper. Arrange all 4 pieces of chicken in the pan and cook until golden brown, about 3 minutes. Flip and cook until light golden brown, about 2 minutes.

3 Meanwhile, in a medium bowl, whisk together the vinegar, mustard, extra-virgin olive oil, and tarragon. Season the vinaigrette with salt and pepper. Add the frisée and red onion and toss to combine. Taste and adjust the seasoning, adding salt and pepper as needed.

4 Put the chicken on plates, top with the salad, and serve.

Pork and apples are another classic pairing, perfect for an autumn feast. This dish marries the crunchy tartness of Granny Smith apples with crispy pan-fried pork. An apple cider vinaigrette fortified with a touch of mustard ties the whole dish together.

BREADED PORK LOIN WITH APPLE SALAD

Serves 4

½ cup all-purpose flour

Kosher salt and freshly ground black pepper

2 **LARGE EGGS**

1 cup panko bread crumbs

4 (6-ounce) pieces **PORK LOIN**, pounded to a ¼-inch thickness

¼ cup olive oil

1 tablespoon Dijon mustard

1 tablespoon honey

¼ cup cider vinegar

½ cup extra-virgin olive oil

2 Granny Smith **APPLES**, cut into matchsticks

1 cup **FRESH FLAT-LEAF PARSLEY** leaves

1 cup thinly sliced **SCALLIONS**, white and green parts

1 Put the flour in a shallow bowl and season well with salt and pepper. Put the eggs in another shallow bowl and beat them lightly. Put the panko in a third shallow bowl and season well with salt and pepper.

2 Put a large skillet over medium-high heat.

3 Season both sides of the pork with salt and pepper. Working with one piece of meat at a time, dredge the pork in the flour, making sure to coat both sides well. Shake off the excess. Dip the pork into the beaten eggs, allowing the excess to drip off. Finally, lay the pork in the panko, turning and pressing to fully coat both sides.

4 Add the olive oil to the preheated pan. Arrange all 4 pieces of pork in the pan and cook for about 2 minutes per side, or until golden brown. If the pan appears too dry, add more oil.

5 Meanwhile, in a medium bowl, whisk together the mustard, honey, vinegar, extra-virgin olive oil, and salt and pepper to taste. Add the apples, parsley, and scallions and toss to combine.

6 Put the pork on plates, top with the apple salad, and serve.

Brussels sprouts are a lot more versatile than we give them credit for. One of my favorite ways to serve them is raw, an approach too many cooks overlook. The secret is to slice them into really thin ribbons and then toss in a flavorful vinaigrette. This dish embraces the homey flavors of a Thanksgiving feast in a meal that takes a fraction of the time to prepare.

TURKEY CUTLET WITH BRUSSELS SPROUT SALAD

Serves 4

½ cup all-purpose flour

Kosher salt and freshly ground black pepper

4 (4-ounce) TURKEY CUTLETS, pounded to a ¼-inch thickness

¼ cup olive oil

½ cup extra-virgin olive oil

¼ cup sherry vinegar

2 tablespoons WHOLE-GRAIN MUSTARD

2 GARLIC cloves, minced

¼ cup chopped FRESH TARRAGON leaves

4 cups thinly sliced BRUSSELS SPROUTS (from ¾ pound)

1 Put a large skillet over medium-high heat.

2 Put the flour in a shallow bowl and season well with salt and pepper. Season both sides of the turkey with salt and pepper. Dredge the turkey in the seasoned flour, shaking off the excess.

3 Add the olive oil to the preheated skillet. Put the turkey in the pan and cook until light golden brown on both sides, about 2 minutes per side.

4 Meanwhile, in a medium bowl, whisk together the extra-virgin olive oil, vinegar, mustard, garlic, tarragon, and a good pinch of salt. Add the shaved Brussels sprouts and toss to combine.

5 Put the turkey cutlets on plates, top with the Brussels sprout salad, and serve.

2 pounds **CHICKEN LIVERS**, cleaned

Kosher salt and freshly ground black pepper

½ cup all-purpose flour

4 tablespoons olive oil

1 cup small-diced **BACON**

½ cup dry **WHITE WINE**

1 cup chicken broth, warmed

2 tablespoons **UNSALTED BUTTER**

2 cups **ARUGULA**

I know a lot of people say they aren't big fans of liver, but chicken livers—cooked right—are magical little devils. Rich, creamy, and earthy, they are one of the best values in the entire grocery store. But overcook them and they turn dry, chalky, and unappetizingly gray. To help prevent overcooking, start with a really hot pan so the livers crisp up quickly.

CHICKEN LIVERS WITH ARUGULA & BACON

Serves 6

1 Put 2 large skillets over medium-high heat.

2 Season both sides of the chicken livers with salt and pepper. Put the flour in a shallow bowl and season well with salt and pepper.

3 To the first pan, add 1 tablespoon of the olive oil and the bacon. Cook until crisp, about 2 minutes. Add the wine and simmer until reduced by half, about 30 seconds. Add the chicken broth and salt and pepper as needed, and continue cooking until reduced by half, about 2 minutes.

4 Meanwhile, to the second pan, add the remaining 3 tablespoons olive oil. Dredge the livers in the seasoned flour, shaking off the excess. Add them to the pan and cook until golden brown, about 1 minute per side. Be careful: Chicken livers tend to spatter while cooking!

5 When the wine mixture has reduced by half, swirl in the butter. Taste and adjust the seasoning, adding salt and pepper as needed. Remove from the heat and stir in the arugula.

6 Put the livers on plates and top with the arugula mixture, spooning the sauce over the top. Serve immediately.

This recipe is a lighter, fresher take on chicken Parmesan. I use white meat like many of the recipes out there, but I swap out the typical melted-cheese-and-tomato-sauce topping for a summery tomato, fresh mozz, and basil salad. I love how the sweet and slightly acidic tomatoes and bright basil cut through the richness of crispy fried chicken.

BREADED CHICKEN BREAST WITH TOMATOES & BASIL

Serves 4

½ cup all-purpose flour

Kosher salt and freshly ground black pepper

3 LARGE EGGS

2 cups plain dry bread crumbs

4 (6-ounce) boneless, skin-on CHICKEN BREAST halves, pounded to a ¼-inch thickness

¼ cup olive oil

¼ cup white balsamic vinegar

½ cup extra-virgin olive oil

2 large TOMATOES, large-diced

½ pound FRESH MOZZARELLA cheese, cut into ½-inch dice

½ cup torn FRESH BASIL leaves

1 Put the flour in a shallow bowl and season well with salt and pepper. Put the eggs in another shallow bowl and beat them lightly. Add the bread crumbs to a third shallow bowl and season well with salt and pepper.

2 Put a large skillet over medium-high heat.

3 Season both sides of the chicken with salt and pepper. Working with one piece of meat at a time, dredge the chicken in the flour, making sure to coat both sides well. Shake off the excess. Dip the chicken into the beaten eggs, allowing the excess to drip off. Finally, lay the chicken in the bread crumbs, turning and pressing to fully coat both sides.

4 Add the olive oil to the preheated pan. Arrange all 4 pieces of chicken in the pan and cook until golden brown, about 3 minutes. Flip and cook until light golden brown, about 2 minutes.

5 Meanwhile, in a medium bowl, whisk together the vinegar and extra-virgin olive oil. Season the vinaigrette with salt and pepper. Add the tomatoes, mozzarella, and basil and toss to combine. Taste and adjust the seasoning, adding salt and pepper as needed.

6 Put the chicken on plates, top with the tomato and mozzarella salad, and serve.

On those rare days when I have a little extra time to enjoy a big breakfast, steak and eggs is always high on my list. By using minute steaks, I can spend less time cooking and more time eating (and maybe have a little time left over for a nap). Otherwise, this is a go-to dinner. The salad is a twist on a warm spinach salad, with the arugula adding a nice peppery bite.

MINUTE STEAK WITH FRIED EGG & WARM ARUGULA SALAD

Serves 4

5 tablespoons olive oil

1 cup diced **BACON**

4 (6-ounce) **MINUTE STEAKS**

Kosher salt and freshly ground black pepper

4 **LARGE EGGS**

1 tablespoon **WHOLE-GRAIN MUSTARD**

¼ cup red wine vinegar

6 cups loosely packed **ARUGULA**

1 Put 2 large skillets over medium-high heat.

2 To the first pan, add 1 tablespoon of the olive oil and then the bacon. Cook until crisp, about 2 minutes.

3 Meanwhile, season both sides of the meat with salt and pepper. Add the remaining 4 tablespoons olive oil to the second pan and add the beef. Cook until the meat browns and the edges begin to curl, about 30 seconds. Flip the beef and cook until the meat is fully cooked, another 30 seconds. Remove the beef to a plate.

4 When the bacon is done, add it and the drippings to a medium bowl, returning the skillet to the heat. To the same skillet, add the eggs, season them with salt and pepper, and cook until the whites are set but the yolks are still runny, about 2 minutes.

5 To the bacon mixture, whisk in the mustard and vinegar. Add the arugula to this dressing and toss to combine. Season with salt and pepper.

6 Top each steak with a fried egg and serve with the warm arugula and bacon salad.

¼ cup olive oil

6 (4-ounce) boneless, skin-on **CHICKEN THIGHS**, pounded to a ¼-inch thickness

Kosher salt and freshly ground black pepper

2 **GARLIC** cloves, sliced

2 tablespoon chopped **FRESH ROSEMARY** leaves

1 (14-ounce) can crushed San Marzano tomatoes with juices

1 cup chopped **KALAMATA OLIVES**

Grated zest and juice of 1 **ORANGE**

Pinch of crushed red pepper flakes

This is the first 5 in 5 recipe I cooked on *The Chew*. The key to this dish is using boneless, skin-on chicken thighs; the skin adds flavor while preventing the meat from drying out. By using boneless thighs and pounding them, they cook so much faster. I love the Mediterranean flavors that come from the garlic, rosemary, and olives.

CHICKEN THIGHS IN TOMATO & OLIVE SAUCE

Serves 6

1 Put a large Dutch oven over medium-high heat. Add the olive oil. Season both sides of the chicken with salt and black pepper. Put the chicken skin-side down in the pan and cook until golden brown, about 2 minutes. Flip the chicken, add the garlic and rosemary, and cook for 30 seconds.

2 Add ½ cup water and deglaze the pan, scraping with a wooden spoon to get up the browned bits on the bottom of the pan. Add the tomatoes with juices, olives, orange zest and juice, and red pepper flakes. Cover and cook until chicken is cooked through, about 2 minutes. Taste and adjust the seasoning, adding salt and black pepper as needed.

3 Remove from the heat and serve.

I always prefer to pair beef dishes with fresh, bright salads rather than heavy hot sides like mashed potatoes. For starters, the acidity of the dressing cuts the richness of the beef, adding another dimension to the dish. And second, I don't feel as guilty eating more beef! Soaking the red onion in vinegar gives it an almost pickled taste and texture. So good!

BREADED BEEF CUTLET WITH SPINACH & MUSHROOM SALAD

Serves 4

½ cup all-purpose flour

Kosher salt and freshly ground black pepper

2 **LARGE EGGS**

1 cup panko bread crumbs

8 (2-ounce) pieces **BEEF SIRLOIN**, pounded to a ¼-inch thickness

½ cup olive oil

1 cup thinly sliced **RED ONION**

2 tablespoons balsamic vinegar

2 cups thinly sliced **BUTTON MUSHROOMS** (from 8 ounces)

6 cups packed **BABY SPINACH**

¼ cup extra-virgin olive oil

1 Put the flour in a shallow bowl and season well with salt and pepper. Put the eggs in another shallow bowl and beat them lightly. Add the panko to a third shallow bowl and season well with salt and pepper.

2 Put 2 large skillets over medium-high heat.

3 Season both sides of the beef with salt and pepper. Working with one piece of meat at a time, dredge the beef in the flour, making sure to coat both sides well. Shake off the excess. Dip the beef into the beaten eggs, allowing the excess to drip off. Finally, lay the beef in the panko, turning and pressing to fully coat both sides.

4 Divide the olive oil between the preheated pans. Put 4 slices of the beef into each pan and cook until golden brown on both sides, about 2 minutes per side.

5 Meanwhile, in a medium bowl, combine the onion, vinegar, and a good pinch of salt. Allow to sit for 1 minute before adding the mushrooms, spinach, and extra-virgin olive oil. Toss well to combine. Taste and adjust the seasoning, adding salt and pepper as needed.

6 Put the beef on plates, top with spinach salad, and serve.

This elegant, classic dish looks and tastes like it's a lot more difficult and time-consuming to prepare than it really is. What makes this so appealing are the buttery, crunchy, toasted almonds. Browning the almonds in the butter really gives the nuts and the entire dish incredible depth and richness.

CHICKEN AMANDINE

Serves 4

4 (6-ounce) boneless, skin-on CHICKEN BREAST halves, pounded to a ¼-inch thickness

Kosher salt and freshly ground black pepper

3 tablespoons olive oil

2 tablespoons UNSALTED BUTTER

½ cup SLICED ALMONDS

Grated zest and juice of 1 ORANGE

¼ cup roughly chopped FRESH FLAT-LEAF PARSLEY leaves

1 Put a large skillet over medium-high heat.

2 Season both sides of the chicken with salt and pepper. Add the olive oil to the preheated pan. Arrange all 4 pieces of chicken in the pan skin-side down and cook until golden brown, about 3 minutes. Flip and cook for 1 minute.

3 Reduce the heat to medium and add the butter and almonds and cook until they just begin to brown, about 30 seconds. Add ½ cup water and the orange zest and juice and cook until slightly reduced, about 30 seconds. Taste and adjust the seasoning, adding salt and pepper as needed.

4 Remove the pan from the heat, stir in the parsley, and serve.

To help me get through the long, cold, and dark winters, I've come up with a few strategies. One of them is cooking dinners with sunny, tropical flavors, like this one. In winter, citrus is at its peak, making dishes like this one all the more appropriate. If I can't always travel to a warm Mediterranean destination, at least I can eat something that reminds me of it!

SHRIMP WITH ORANGE & PINE NUTS

Serves 4

1 pound shelled and deveined **LARGE SHRIMP** (16 to 20)

Kosher salt and freshly ground black pepper

3 tablespoons olive oil

2 tablespoons **UNSALTED BUTTER**

¼ cup **PINE NUTS**

Grated zest and juice of 1 **ORANGE**

1 tablespoon sherry vinegar

¼ cup chopped **FRESH FLAT-LEAF PARSLEY** leaves

1 Put a large skillet over medium heat.

2 Season the shrimp with salt and pepper. Add the olive oil to the preheated pan, then add the shrimp. Cook until the shrimp begin to turn pink, about 1 minute. Flip the shrimp, then add the butter and pine nuts. Cook until the pine nuts begin to turn light golden brown and the shrimp are just cooked through, about 1 minute.

3 Add the orange zest and juice, the vinegar, and parsley and stir to combine. Taste and adjust the seasoning, adding salt and pepper as needed. Serve immediately.

4 (6-ounce) **TROUT FILLETS**, skin removed

Kosher salt and freshly ground black pepper

4 tablespoons olive oil

1 pound **GREEN BEANS**

½ cup **SLICED ALMONDS**

2 tablespoons **UNSALTED BUTTER**

Juice of 1 **LEMON**

Something magical happens when you put buttery toasted almond slices on top of pretty much anything. That's how so many moms got their kids to eat veggies like green beans! Don't skip the step of drying the trout on paper towels, because it really helps the fish to develop a nice crust in the pan—and that's the best part!

TROUT & GREEN BEANS

Serves 4

1 Put 2 large skillets over medium-high heat.

2 Using paper towels, pat dry the trout fillets. Season the fish on both sides with salt and pepper.

3 To the first skillet, add 2 tablespoons of the olive oil. When the oil is hot, add the green beans and a large pinch each of salt and pepper, and cook until the beans turn bright green and begin to soften, about 2 minutes. Add the almonds and cook until they just begin to brown, about 1 minute. Add the butter and stir. Taste and adjust the seasoning, adding salt and pepper as needed. Reduce the heat to low to keep warm.

4 Meanwhile, to the second skillet, add the remaining 2 tablespoons olive oil. Put the fish in the pan and cook until the fish is golden brown, 2 to 3 minutes. Flip the fish, reduce the heat to medium-low, and cook until cooked through, about 2 minutes. Drizzle the fish with the lemon juice and remove from the heat.

5 Put the fish on plates, spoon the green beans alongside, and serve.

½ cup all-purpose flour

Kosher salt and freshly ground black pepper

6 (4-ounce) boneless, skinless **CHICKEN THIGHS**, pounded to a ¼-inch thickness

¼ cup olive oil

3 cups sliced stemmed **SHIITAKE MUSHROOMS**

1 **GARLIC** clove, minced

¼ cup Marsala wine

2 tablespoons **UNSALTED BUTTER**

¼ cup finely chopped **FRESH FLAT-LEAF PARSLEY** leaves

This dish is so popular for a reason: It has a uniquely appealing flavor that comes from Marsala wine. I know most people usually don't have a bottle of Marsala lying around, but if you love this dish—and I think you will—I suggest adding a bottle to your pantry. Unlike regular wine, Marsala will last opened for weeks. Feel free to use sweet or dry Marsala according to your personal taste. Me, I like sweet here.

CHICKEN MARSALA

Serves 6

1 Put a large skillet over medium-high heat.

2 Put the flour in a shallow bowl and season with salt and pepper. Season both sides of the chicken with salt and pepper. Dredge the chicken in the seasoned flour, shaking off the excess.

3 Add the olive oil to the preheated pan. Add the chicken and cook until golden brown, about 2 minutes. Flip the chicken and scoot the pieces to one side of the pan. Add the mushrooms and garlic to the empty space and cook until the garlic is fragrant and the mushrooms begin to soften, about 1 minute.

4 Add the Marsala and deglaze the pan, scraping with a wooden spoon to get up the browned bits on the bottom of the pan. Stir to combine everything in the pan. Add ¼ cup water and cook until the liquid is reduced by half, another minute. Remove from the heat and stir in the butter and parsley. Taste and adjust the seasoning, adding salt and pepper as needed.

5 Put the chicken on plates, spoon the sauce on top, and serve.

6 (4-ounce) pieces PORK TENDERLOIN

6 FRESH SAGE leaves

6 thin slices PROSCIUTTO

½ cup all-purpose flour

Kosher salt and freshly ground black pepper

¼ cup olive oil

2 tablespoons UNSALTED BUTTER

4 cups loosely packed ARUGULA

Veal Saltimbocca is a classic Roman dish that layers tender veal, salty prosciutto, and woodsy sage for an explosion of flavors and textures. This version swaps out the veal for pork, which is not only far less expensive, but also results in pork-on-pork goodness, always a good thing in my book!

PORK SALTIMBOCCA

Serves 6

1 Put a large skillet over medium-high heat.

2 Put a large piece of plastic wrap on a cutting board. Arrange all of the pork pieces on the plastic wrap so they do not overlap. On top of each piece of pork, put 1 sage leaf and then top with 1 slice prosciutto (folded if necessary). Cover all of the pork with another large piece of plastic wrap and lightly pound the piles with a meat mallet to flatten the meat and help the ingredients stick together.

3 Put the flour in a shallow bowl and season with salt and pepper. Season both sides of the pork bundles with salt and pepper. Dredge them in the seasoned flour, shaking off the excess.

4 Add the olive oil to the preheated pan. Add the pork bundles and cook until light golden brown, about 2 minutes per side. Add ½ cup water and deglaze the pan, scraping with a wooden spoon to get up the browned bits on the bottom of the pan. Cook until the liquid is reduced by half, another minute. Taste and add salt and pepper as needed.

5 Remove the pan from the heat, move the pork to one side of the pan, and add the butter, swirling it around in the pan until fully melted. Stir in the arugula and serve immediately.

2 tablespoons cornstarch

2 cups beef broth

1 pound **GROUND BEEF** (80% lean)

¼ cup plain dry bread crumbs

1 **LARGE EGG**

½ cup plus 3 tablespoons canned tomato sauce

4 tablespoons Worcestershire sauce

Kosher salt and freshly ground black pepper

3 tablespoons olive oil

1 large **YELLOW ONION**, thinly sliced (2 cups)

As a kid, Salisbury steak was my least favorite school lunch of them all. Gray and tasteless meat buried in a bland and lumpy gravy. *Gross!* Later on, when I became a chef, I gave the dish another shot. This is the version I came up with—and it's delicious, like mini-meatloaf patties in a rich, oniony gravy. If you really want to be nostalgic, serve it with peas and mashed potatoes for the full school-lunch effect.

SALISBURY STEAK

Serves 4

1 In a small bowl, whisk together the cornstarch and ¼ cup of the beef broth.

2 Put a large skillet over medium-high heat.

3 In a large bowl, combine the beef, bread crumbs, egg, 3 tablespoons of the tomato sauce, 3 tablespoons of the Worcestershire sauce, 1 teaspoon salt, and ½ teaspoon pepper. Mix thoroughly and then divide the mixture into 4 equal portions. Shape each portion into a flat oval-shaped patty, about ¼ inch thick. Season both sides of the patties with salt and pepper.

4 Add the olive oil to the preheated skillet. Add the beef patties and cook until golden brown, about 2 minutes. Flip the meat and scoot the patties to one side of the pan. Add the onion and a pinch each of salt and pepper to the empty space and cook until the beef patties are golden brown on the second side, about 2 minutes. Put the patties on a plate and cover with foil while you prepare the sauce.

5 To the same skillet, add the remaining 1¾ cups beef broth, ½ cup tomato sauce, and 1 tablespoon Worcestershire sauce and bring to a boil. Whisk in the cornstarch mixture. Taste and adjust the seasoning, adding salt and pepper as needed. Return the beef patties to the pan, and cook until the sauce thickens and the meat is warmed through, about 1 minute.

6 Remove from the heat and serve.

I prefer to eat my veggies in season, even though most are now available year round. But just because you can *find* asparagus in winter, doesn't mean it *tastes* like it does in spring. Hardly! So please save this recipe for spring, when you start seeing those beautiful green shoots appearing at your farmers' market.

GARLIC CHICKEN WITH ASPARAGUS

Serves 4

¼ cup olive oil

4 (4-ounce) boneless, skin-on CHICKEN THIGHS, pounded to a ¼-inch thickness

Kosher salt and freshly ground black pepper

4 GARLIC cloves, minced

1 bunch ASPARAGUS, cut crosswise into 1-inch pieces

Pinch of crushed red pepper flakes

¼ cup chopped FRESH FLAT-LEAF PARSLEY leaves

Grated zest and juice of 2 LEMONS

2 tablespoons extra-virgin olive oil

1 Put a large Dutch oven over medium-high heat. Add the olive oil. Season both sides of the chicken with salt and black pepper. Put the chicken skin-side down in the pan and cook until golden brown, about 2 minutes. Flip the chicken, add the garlic, and cook for 30 seconds.

2 Add 1 cup water and deglaze the pan, scraping with a wooden spoon to get up the browned bits on the bottom of the pan. Add the asparagus, red pepper flakes, and a pinch of salt. Cover and cook until the asparagus is crisp-tender, about 2 minutes.

3 Remove from the heat and stir in the parsley, lemon zest and juice, and extra-virgin olive oil. Serve immediately.

In summer, when peaches are in season, I look for every which way to prepare them. In my first cookbook, *Live to Cook*, I did a roasted rack of pork with grilled peaches, an impressive and delicious dish that takes considerably longer than 5 minutes to prepare. This recipe is much, much easier, but it still combines two of my favorite things: pork and peaches.

PORK CUTLET WITH PEACHES & ALMONDS

Serves 6

½ cup all-purpose flour

Kosher salt and freshly ground black pepper

6 (4-ounce) pieces **PORK TENDERLOIN**, pounded to a ¼-inch thickness

¼ cup olive oil

2 tablespoons **UNSALTED BUTTER**

1 cup **SLIVERED ALMONDS**

2 **PEACHES**, sliced

2 tablespoons sherry vinegar

¼ cup chopped **FRESH FLAT-LEAF PARSLEY** leaves

1 Put a large skillet over medium-high heat.

2 Put the flour in a shallow bowl and season with salt and pepper. Season both sides of the pork with salt and pepper. Dredge the pork in the seasoned flour, shaking off the excess.

3 Add the olive oil to the preheated pan. Add the pork to the pan and cook until golden brown, about 2 minutes. Flip the meat and cook until light golden brown, about 1 minute. Add the butter and almonds and cook until the almonds turn golden brown, about 1 minute.

4 Add ½ cup water and deglaze the pan, scraping with a wooden spoon to get up the browned bits on the bottom of the pan. Cook until the liquid is reduced by half, another 1 minute. Taste and adjust the seasoning, adding salt and pepper as needed.

5 Remove the pan from the heat and stir in the peaches, vinegar, and parsley. Serve immediately.

Browning butter totally transforms its flavor, giving it a deep, rich, nutty quality. When paired with woodsy sage, it tastes even better. To counter all those low notes are the tart and briny capers and the bright lemon. I learned how to make this dish years ago and haven't stopped making it since.

TURKEY CUTLET WITH LEMON, CAPERS & BROWN BUTTER

Serves 4

4 (4-ounce) TURKEY CUTLETS, pounded to a ¼-inch thickness

Kosher salt and freshly ground black pepper

2 tablespoons olive oil

2 tablespoons UNSALTED BUTTER

⅓ cup finely chopped FRESH SAGE leaves

2 tablespoons capers, rinsed and drained

Juice of 1 LEMON

1 Put a large skillet over medium-high heat.

2 Season both sides of the turkey with salt and pepper. Add the olive oil to the preheated pan. Arrange all 4 pieces of turkey in the pan and cook until light golden brown, about 2 minutes. Flip and cook until light golden brown, about 1 minute. Reduce the heat to medium and add the butter. When the butter is fully melted and begins to brown, add the sage, capers, lemon juice, and ¼ cup water. Cook until the sauce reduces slightly, about 1 minute.

3 Put the turkey on plates, spoon the sauce on top, and serve.

½ cup all-purpose flour

Kosher salt and freshly ground black pepper

3 **LARGE EGGS**

2 cups plain dry bread crumbs

4 (6-ounce) boneless, skinless **CHICKEN BREAST** halves, pounded to a ¼-inch thickness

¼ cup olive oil

1 large **TOMATO**, cut into 4 slices

½ pound **FRESH MOZZARELLA** cheese, cut into ¼-inch-thick slices

½ cup torn **FRESH BASIL** leaves

I got hooked on this dish when I was chef at Giovanni's Ristorante in Cleveland twenty years ago. I must have had it for lunch every other day of the week! This Italian staple is typically made with veal cutlets, which are not very thrifty! My version uses chicken breasts, a much more economical ingredient. I find that if you pound out the chicken and don't cook it to death, you can still have tender, delicious results.

CHICKEN MILANESE

Serves 4

1 Put the flour in a shallow bowl and season well with salt and pepper. Put the eggs in another shallow bowl and beat them lightly. Add the bread crumbs to a third shallow bowl and season well with salt and pepper.

2 Put a large Dutch oven over medium-high heat.

3 Season both sides of the chicken with salt and pepper. Dredge each piece of meat in the flour, coating both sides well. Shake off the excess. Dip the chicken into the beaten eggs, allowing the excess to drip off. Finally, coat the chicken in the bread crumbs.

4 Pour the oil into the pan. Add the chicken and cook until golden brown, about 3 minutes. Flip and cook until light golden brown, about 1 minute. Reduce the heat to medium and top each piece of chicken with 1 tomato slice and some mozzarella. Season with salt and pepper, cover the pan, and cook until the cheese melts, about 1 minute.

5 Put the chicken on plates, top with the basil, and serve.

Chicken Diablo—aka the devil's chicken—gets its name from its demonic heat level. Depending on the spiciness of the jalapeño pepper, this dish can range anywhere from mild to medium. But if you like things super-spicy, like my stepson, Kyle, go ahead and add another jalapeño or, if you're really brave, a habanero.

CHICKEN DIABLO

Serves 6

¼ cup olive oil

6 (4-ounce) boneless, skin-on CHICKEN THIGHS, pounded to a ¼-inch thickness

Kosher salt and freshly ground black pepper

2 GARLIC cloves, sliced

1 RED BELL PEPPER, thinly sliced

1 JALAPEÑO, sliced into rings

1 (14-ounce) can San Marzano tomatoes with juices

2 tablespoons capers, rinsed and drained

½ cup roughly chopped FRESH FLAT-LEAF PARSLEY leaves

1 Put a Dutch oven over medium-high heat.

2 Add the olive oil to the preheated pan. Season both sides of the chicken with salt and pepper. Put the chicken skin-side down in the pan and cook until golden brown, about 2 minutes. Flip the chicken and cook for another 30 seconds. Add the garlic, bell pepper, jalapeño, and a pinch of salt, and cook for another 30 seconds.

3 Add ½ cup water and deglaze the pan, scraping with a wooden spoon to get up the browned bits on the bottom of the pan. Cook until the liquid is reduced by half, another minute. Add the tomatoes with juices and capers, cover the pan, and cook for 2 minutes.

4 Remove the pan from the heat and stir in the parsley. Taste and adjust the seasoning, adding salt and pepper as needed. Serve immediately.

In Cleveland, we know and love our *Wienerschnitzel*, which is served at countless Eastern European restaurants. Typically, the dish is made with veal, but I almost always prefer pork. And guess what? It is much more affordable! We put this dish on the lunch menu at Lola when we first opened and we've been serving some version of it ever since.

PORK SCHNITZEL

Serves 4

½ cup all-purpose flour

Kosher salt and freshly ground black pepper

2 **LARGE EGGS**

2 cups plain dry bread crumbs

4 (4-ounce) pieces **PORK TENDERLOIN**, pounded to a ¼-inch thickness

½ cup olive oil

2 tablespoons Dijon mustard

½ cup extra-virgin olive oil

Grated zest and juice of 2 **LEMONS**

1 **GRANNY SMITH APPLE**, cut into matchsticks

3 cups loosely packed **ARUGULA**

1 Put the flour in a shallow bowl and season well with salt and pepper. Put the eggs in another shallow bowl and beat them lightly. Add the bread crumbs to a third shallow bowl and season well with salt and pepper.

2 Put a large skillet over medium-high heat.

3 Season both sides of the pork with salt and pepper. Working with one piece of meat at a time, dredge the pork in the flour, making sure to coat both sides well. Shake off the excess. Dip the pork into the beaten eggs, allowing the excess to drip off. Finally, lay the pork in the bread crumbs, turning and pressing to fully coat both sides.

4 Add the olive oil to the preheated pan. Arrange all 4 pieces of pork in the pan and cook until golden brown, about 3 minutes. Flip and cook until light golden brown, about 2 minutes.

5 Meanwhile, in a medium bowl, whisk together the mustard, extra-virgin olive oil, and lemon zest and juice. Season the vinaigrette with salt and pepper. Add the apples and arugula and toss to combine.

6 Put the pork on plates, top with the apple salad, and serve.

You can pretty much find snow peas (not the plumper sweet or sugar snap peas) all year round, making this dish a fine midwinter, midweek meal. If you haven't noticed, I love using fresh citrus juice and zest because it adds such a bright and sunny note to everything it touches. Don't overcook the snow pea slivers—you want them to retain some crunch.

CHICKEN WITH SNOW PEAS & RED PEPPER FLAKES

Serves 4

½ cup all-purpose flour

Kosher salt and freshly ground black pepper

4 (4-ounce) boneless, skin-on CHICKEN THIGHS, pounded to a ¼-inch thickness

¼ cup olive oil

2 GARLIC cloves, sliced

2 tablespoons sesame seeds

Grated zest and juice of 2 ORANGES

¼ teaspoon crushed red pepper flakes

½ pound SNOW PEAS, thinly sliced (3 cups)

2 tablespoons UNSALTED BUTTER

1 Put a large Dutch oven over medium-high heat.

2 Put the flour in a shallow bowl and season with salt and pepper. Season both sides of the chicken with salt and pepper. Dredge the chicken in the seasoned flour, shaking off the excess.

3 Pour the oil into the pan. Add all 4 pieces of chicken skin-side down and cook until golden brown, about 2 minutes. Flip the chicken, add the garlic, sesame seeds, and a pinch of salt, and cook for 30 seconds.

4 Add ½ cup water and deglaze the pan, scraping with a wooden spoon to get up the browned bits on the bottom of the pan. Simmer until the liquid is reduced by half, 1 minute. Add the orange zest and juice and red pepper flakes, cover the pan, and cook for 1 minute. Add the snow peas, cover, and cook until slightly tender, about 1 minute.

5 Remove the pan from the heat and add the butter, swirling it around in the pan until fully melted. Taste and adjust the seasoning, adding salt and black pepper as needed. Serve immediately.

½ cup all-purpose flour

½ tablespoon paprika

Kosher salt and freshly ground black pepper

6 (4-ounce) **CUBE STEAKS**

3 tablespoons cornstarch

2 cups **BEEF BROTH**

4 tablespoons olive oil

1 large **YELLOW ONION**, thinly sliced (2 cups)

3 **GARLIC** cloves, minced

1 (14-ounce) can diced San Marzano tomatoes with juices

Cube steaks are an affordable alternative to pricier cuts of meat, and they still have great beefy flavor. Usually they are cut from top round or top sirloin that has been run through a tenderizing machine. The meat comes out the other end perforated and square-shaped, which is how cube steaks get their name.

SWISS STEAK

Serves 6

1 Put a large skillet over medium-high heat.

2 Put the flour in a shallow bowl and season with the paprika and salt and pepper. Season both sides of the cube steaks with salt and pepper. Dredge the meat in the seasoned flour, shaking off the excess.

3 In a small bowl, whisk together the cornstarch and ½ cup of the beef broth.

4 Add 3 tablespoons of the olive oil to the preheated skillet. Put the cube steaks in the pan and cook until light golden brown on both sides, about 1 minute per side. Remove to a platter when done.

5 Add the remaining 1 tablespoon olive oil to the skillet followed by the onion, garlic, and a pinch of salt. Cook until the onions start to soften and caramelize, about 1 minute. Stir in the tomatoes with juices and remaining 1½ cups beef broth and bring to a boil.

6 Whisk in the cornstarch mixture. Taste and adjust the seasoning, adding salt and pepper as needed. Reduce the heat to medium-low, return the steaks to the pan, and cook until the sauce thickens and the meat is warmed through, about 1 minute.

7 Remove from the heat and serve.

If you're looking to add a little spice to your life, start with this recipe. I make this dish pretty frequently because Liz loves it. We usually whip up a batch of coconut rice and serve the beef right on top. The sweet coconut does a great job of taming the heat. If you can't find tri-tip, go ahead and substitute sirloin.

BEEF TRI-TIP WITH SPICY PEPPERS

Serves 4

½ cup all-purpose flour

Kosher salt and freshly ground black pepper

4 (4-ounce) BEEF TRI-TIP STEAKS

¼ cup olive oil

2 RED BELL PEPPERS, thinly sliced

1 JALAPEÑO, thinly sliced into rings

1 teaspoon coriander seeds, toasted and ground

Grated zest and juice of 2 LIMES

1 cup FRESH BASIL leaves, torn

1 Put a large skillet over medium-high heat.

2 Put the flour in a shallow bowl and season with salt and pepper. Season both sides of the beef with salt and pepper. Dredge the beef in the seasoned flour, shaking off the excess.

3 Add the olive oil to the preheated pan. Add the beef and cook until light golden brown, about 2 minutes. Flip the meat and scoot the steaks to one side of the pan. Add the bell peppers, jalapeño, coriander, and a good pinch of salt to the empty space and cook until softened and slightly caramelized, about 1 minute.

4 Add ½ cup water and deglaze the skillet, scraping with a wooden spoon to get up the browned bits on the bottom of the pan. Cook until the liquid is reduced by half, about 1 minute.

5 Remove the pan from the heat, stir in the lime zest and juice and basil, and serve.

2 tablespoons soy sauce

Grated zest and juice of 2 **LIMES**

¼ teaspoon crushed red pepper flakes

1 teaspoon sugar

¼ cup olive oil

6 (4-ounce) pieces **PORK TENDERLOIN**, pounded to a ¼-inch thickness

Kosher salt and freshly ground black pepper

4 cups **BROCCOLI** florets (from 1 large head)

½ cup crushed **PEANUTS**

¼ cup **FRESH CILANTRO** leaves

You don't need to order in Chinese food to satisfy your stir-fry craving. It is so easy to make stir-fries at home that taste fresher and use a whole lot less oil, salt, and sugar. I think the cilantro is what gives this dish its characteristic Asian flavor, but if you or somebody in your family doesn't like it, go ahead and substitute fresh basil or flat-leaf parsley.

PORK & BROCCOLI STIR-FRY

Serves 6

1 Put a large Dutch oven over medium-high heat.

2 In a small bowl, whisk together the soy sauce, lime zest and juice, red pepper flakes, and sugar.

3 Add the olive oil to the preheated pan. Season both sides of the pork with salt and black pepper. Arrange all 6 pieces of pork in the pan and cook until golden brown, about 2 minutes. Flip the pork and scoot the pieces to one side of the pan. Add the broccoli, peanuts, and a pinch of salt to the empty space and cook for 1 minute.

4 Add ½ cup water and deglaze the pan, scraping with a wooden spoon to get up the browned bits on the bottom of the pan. Cover the pan and cook for 1 minute. Add the soy sauce mixture, cover, and cook until slightly reduced, about 30 seconds.

5 Remove from the heat and stir in the cilantro. Taste and adjust the seasoning, adding salt and black pepper as needed. Serve immediately.

I know everybody loves meat and potatoes—it's pretty much our national dish—but I rarely pair the two foods, finding them too heavy together. I do make an exception for this recipe, however—especially on a chilly winter's night. There is just something so comforting about beef and mushrooms in a rich wine sauce served over a mound of buttery mashed potatoes. I love using tri-tip because it cooks up fast and has great flavor.

BEEF TRI-TIP WITH MUSHROOM SAUCE

Serves 4

4 (4-ounce) BEEF TRI-TIP STEAKS

Kosher salt and freshly ground black pepper

3 tablespoons olive oil

3 cups thinly sliced CREMINI MUSHROOMS

2 GARLIC cloves, minced

¼ cup dry red wine

1 tablespoon chopped FRESH ROSEMARY leaves

2 tablespoons UNSALTED BUTTER

1 Put a large skillet over medium-high heat.

2 Season both sides of the beef with salt and pepper. Add the olive oil to the preheated pan. Add the beef and cook until light golden brown, about 2 minutes. Flip the meat and scoot the pieces to one side of the pan. Add the mushrooms, garlic, and a good pinch of salt to the empty space and cook until softened and slightly caramelized, about 1 minute.

3 Add the red wine and deglaze the pan, scraping with a wooden spoon to get up the browned bits on the bottom of the pan. Add ¼ cup water and the rosemary and cook until the liquid is reduced by half, another minute.

4 Remove the pan from the heat, stir in the butter, and serve.

Brown—*not burnt!*—butter is such an underused flavor in home kitchens. As butter cooks, it goes from foamy and pale yellow to a rich golden brown. And the taste and aroma change too, going from mild and sweet to nutty and complex. I love how the fresh orange in this recipe plays against those deeper flavors, but you can use brown butter in everything from mashed potatoes to fudge brownies!

CHICKEN WITH BROWN BUTTER & ORANGE

Serves 4

½ cup all-purpose flour

Kosher salt and freshly ground black pepper

4 (6-ounce) boneless, skin-on **CHICKEN BREAST** halves, pounded to a ¼-inch thickness

3 tablespoons olive oil

4 tablespoons **UNSALTED BUTTER**

½ cup **SLICED ALMONDS**

Grated zest and juice of 1 **ORANGE**

¼ cup roughly chopped **FRESH FLAT-LEAF PARSLEY** leaves

1 Put a large skillet over medium-high heat.

2 Put the flour in a shallow bowl and season with salt and pepper. Season both sides of the chicken with salt and pepper. Dredge the chicken in the seasoned flour, shaking off the excess.

3 Add the olive oil to the preheated pan. Add the chicken to the pan and cook until golden brown, about 2 minutes. Flip the meat and cook until light golden brown, about 1 minute. Add the butter and almonds and cook until the butter turns golden brown and the almonds are toasted, about 1 minute.

4 Remove the pan from the heat and stir in the orange zest and juice and parsley. Serve immediately.

BRICKED GRILLED CHICKEN WITH WHITE BEAN SALAD 183

GRILLED SALMON & AVOCADO SALAD 185

GRILLED CHICKEN BREASTS WITH OLIVE & ORANGE SALAD 186

SHRIMP WITH GRILLED LEMON & MINT 187

GRILLED ROMAINE & ANCHOVY SALAD WITH EGG 188

GRILLED SWORDFISH & PEPPER SALAD 191

GRILLED EGGPLANT WITH MOZZARELLA SALAD 192

7
LET'S GRILL

GRILLED SALMON WITH CARROT & PEANUT SALAD 193

GRILLED FLANK STEAK WITH CORN & BACON SALAD 196

GRILLED CHICKEN WITH LEMON COUSCOUS SALAD 199

GRILLED SKIRT STEAK WITH CHICKPEA SALAD 200

GRILLED SHRIMP & GRAPEFRUIT SALAD 203

GRILLED SALMON & SHAVED ZUCCHINI SALAD 204

GRILLED SKIRT STEAK WITH PARSLEY SAUCE 206

GRILLED SALMON WITH SHAVED CUCUMBERS 207

GRILLED HAM STEAK WITH FIGS & ARUGULA 209

I ENJOY COOKING OVER A LIVE FIRE so much that I've been known to shovel a path in the snow just to get to the grill.

Grilling gives meat, fish, vegetables, and even fruit such a wonderful charred, smoky flavor that it's worth the effort even in lousy weather. And by cooking outdoors, you don't heat up or mess up the kitchen!

Grilling is the natural choice when hosting friends or family, too. Depending on how large your grill is, you can easily double or triple these recipes to feed a large crowd. Like all the recipes in this book, this section is loaded with meals that take no time to cook, leaving you more time to spend with your guests. And cleanup is a breeze. Just make sure you have all your utensils, ingredients, and platters ready to go.

If you are using charcoal, you'll need to give it plenty of time to reach the proper burning temperature. Gas grills, too, need at least twenty minutes to preheat. Make sure you start with a clean and oiled grill grate to prevent the food from sticking. The easiest time to clean and oil the grate is when it is good and hot. Just be careful!

While I prefer grilling over a live fire, I know that not everyone has access to a grill. (Or aren't as crazy as me and willing to grill in snow boots.) These recipes work fine in a grill pan; you just won't get those amazing smoky flavors. Make sure you allow the pan to get very hot. Regardless of which equipment you use, remember to leave the food alone after putting it in the pan or on the grill. Don't poke it or flip it for a few minutes, so the food has time to develop a crust and release from the pan or grate. If you need something to do, drink a beer!

This method of cooking a chicken is not only fast but it also helps give the meat a really crisp crust. Simply take two regular bricks and wrap them in aluminum foil. If you don't have any bricks, you can use heavy cans from the pantry. The combination of crisp yet moist chicken, creamy cannellini beans, and bright olives and parsley is great year round.

BRICKED GRILLED CHICKEN WITH WHITE BEAN SALAD

Serves 4

4 (4-ounce) boneless, skin-on **CHICKEN THIGHS**, pounded thin

Kosher salt and freshly ground black pepper

2 tablespoons olive oil

2 tablespoons red wine vinegar

2 **GARLIC** cloves, minced

3 tablespoons extra-virgin olive oil

1 (15-ounce) can cannellini or white beans, rinsed and drained

1 cup quartered **CHERRY TOMATOES**

½ cup halved pitted **KALAMATA OLIVES**

¼ cup chopped **FRESH FLAT-LEAF PARSLEY** leaves

1 Preheat a grill or grill pan to medium-high heat.

2 Season the chicken on both sides with salt and pepper. Drizzle with the olive oil and put skin-side down on the grill. Using 2 bricks, put 1 brick on top of 2 thighs, cover the grill, and cook until nicely charred and the chicken releases from the grill, about 3 minutes. Remove the bricks, flip the chicken, and return the bricks to the meat. Cover the grill and cook until cooked through, about 2 minutes.

3 Meanwhile, in a medium bowl, whisk together the vinegar, garlic, and extra-virgin olive oil. Add the beans, tomatoes, olives, and parsley and toss to combine. Taste and adjust the seasoning, adding salt and pepper as needed.

4 Put the chicken on plates, top with the white bean salad, and serve.

4 (6-ounce) skinless SALMON STEAKS

Kosher salt and freshly ground black pepper

1 tablespoon chipotle powder

2 tablespoons olive oil

Grated zest and juice of 2 LIMES

½ cup thinly sliced RED ONION

¼ cup chopped FRESH CILANTRO leaves

6 tablespoons extra-virgin olive oil

1 AVOCADO, sliced

1 Preheat a grill or grill pan to medium-high heat.

2 Season the salmon on both sides with salt, pepper, and the chipotle powder. Drizzle with the olive oil and put on the grill. Cook until nicely charred and the fish releases from the grill, about 3 minutes, then flip, and cook until medium-rare, about 2 minutes. If you prefer your fish to be cooked past medium-rare, cover the grill while cooking.

3 Meanwhile, in a medium bowl, stir together the lime zest and juice, onion, cilantro, extra-virgin olive oil, and a good pinch of salt. Taste and adjust the seasoning, adding salt and pepper as needed. Add the sliced avocado and toss gently to coat the avocado.

4 Remove the salmon from the grill, top with avocado salad, and serve.

This is the perfect summertime dish; it's light, refreshing, and a wee bit tropical. I recommend not cooking the salmon past medium-rare as it actually gets fishier tasting the longer you cook it. The avocado salad gives the dish a nice creaminess, which complements the meaty fish.

GRILLED SALMON & AVOCADO SALAD

Serves 4

Orange and olives are one of those great Mediterranean flavor combinations that just work so well together. Here I pair them with grilled chicken, but this dish would work equally well with grilled fish or pork. Try this recipe in the dead of winter for a nice pick-me-up thanks to the bright mint and dill.

GRILLED CHICKEN BREAST WITH OLIVE & ORANGE SALAD

Serves 4

4 (6-ounce) boneless, skin-on CHICKEN BREAST halves

Kosher salt and freshly ground black pepper

2 tablespoons olive oil

6 tablespoons extra-virgin olive oil

2 tablespoons sherry vinegar

2 NAVEL ORANGES, peeled and cut into wheels, or separated into segments (see page 203)

¼ cup halved pitted KALAMATA OLIVES

¼ cup torn FRESH MINT leaves

2 tablespoons roughly chopped FRESH DILL

1 Preheat a grill or grill pan to medium-high heat.

2 Season the chicken on both sides with salt and pepper. Drizzle with the olive oil and put the chicken skin-side down on the grill. Cover and cook until nicely charred and the chicken releases from the grill, about 3 minutes. Flip the chicken, cover, and cook until cooked through, about 2 minutes.

3 Meanwhile, in a medium bowl, whisk together the extra-virgin olive oil and vinegar. Season with salt and pepper. Add the oranges, olives, mint, and dill and stir to combine.

4 Put the chicken on plates, spoon the salad on top, and serve.

Grilling lemons is another simple way to up the flavor of everyday ingredients. When lemons get a sweet, caramelized crust, they transform from one-note wonders to a symphony of flavors. When paired with grilled shrimp and summery mint, the result is almost magical.

SHRIMP WITH GRILLED LEMON & MINT

Serves 4

2 **LEMONS**, halved

½ cup plus 1 tablespoon olive oil

¼ cup sherry vinegar

2 **GARLIC** cloves, minced

1 **JALAPEÑO**, seeds and ribs removed, finely chopped

½ teaspoon coriander seeds, toasted and ground

Kosher salt and freshly ground black pepper

1 pound shelled and deveined **LARGE SHRIMP**

¼ cup torn **FRESH MINT** leaves

1 Preheat a grill or grill pan to medium-high heat.

2 Drizzle the cut sides of the lemons with 1 tablespoon of the olive oil and grill, cut-side down, until nicely charred, about 4 minutes.

3 Meanwhile, in a medium bowl, whisk together the vinegar, garlic, jalapeño, coriander, and remaining ½ cup olive oil. Season with salt and pepper. Add the shrimp to the vinaigrette and marinate for 2 minutes.

4 Put the shrimp on the grill and cook until pink, about 2 minutes per side.

5 Remove the shrimp from the grill and put them on plates. Squeeze the lemons over top, garnish with mint, and serve.

I know grilling lettuce probably sounds weird, but, like with fruit, cooking intensifies the natural sweetness and flavor—and you get the added benefit of those smoky undertones. What you end up with here is like a grilled Caesar salad. Try to find white anchovies, which are sweeter, firmer, and way more delicious than those puny, dark, tinned ones.

GRILLED ROMAINE & ANCHOVY SALAD WITH EGG

Serves 6

12 **WHITE ANCHOVIES**, minced

2 **GARLIC** cloves, minced

2 tablespoons Dijon mustard

2 tablespoons plain dry bread crumbs

½ cup olive oil

Kosher salt and freshly ground black pepper

3 **HEARTS OF ROMAINE**, split lengthwise

1 tablespoon **UNSALTED BUTTER**

4 **LARGE EGGS**

1 Preheat a grill or grill pan to medium-high heat. Put a medium skillet over medium heat.

2 In a small bowl, mix the anchovies, garlic, mustard, bread crumbs, olive oil, and salt and pepper to taste. Rub this mixture onto both sides of the romaine halves. Put the romaine cut-side down on the grill and cook until lightly charred but still crisp, about 2 minutes. Flip and cook until lightly charred, another minute.

3 Meanwhile, add the butter to the preheated skillet. When the butter has melted, crack all 4 eggs into the pan and season with salt and pepper. Cook sunny-side up until the whites are set but the yolks are still runny, about 2 minutes.

4 Remove the romaine from the grill, top with the sunny-side-up eggs, and serve.

For the longest time, swordfish was overfished, overconsumed, and in danger of going away forever. But thanks to conservation and management practices, the fish has made a comeback—and that's great news because it has always been one of my favorites. The firm, meaty fish can stand up to some pretty bold flavors, like this kicky pepper salad.

GRILLED SWORDFISH & PEPPER SALAD

Serves 4

4 (5-ounce) SWORDFISH STEAKS

Kosher salt and freshly ground black pepper

16 tablespoons olive oil

6 tablespoons sherry vinegar

1 RED BELL PEPPER, thinly sliced

1 JALAPEÑO, thinly sliced

½ cup thinly sliced RED ONION

1 cup torn FRESH BASIL leaves

1 Preheat a grill or grill pan to high heat.

2 Season the swordfish on both sides with salt and pepper. Drizzle with 4 tablespoons of the olive oil and put on the grill. Cover and cook until nicely charred and the fish releases from the grill, about 3 minutes. Flip, cover, and cook until cooked through, about 2 minutes.

3 Meanwhile, in a medium bowl, whisk together the vinegar, remaining 12 tablespoons olive oil, and salt and black pepper to taste. Add the bell pepper, jalapeño, onion, and basil and toss to combine.

4 Remove the swordfish from the grill, top with pepper salad and a few spoonfuls of vinaigrette from the bowl, and serve.

Eggplant Parmesan, like chicken Parmesan, is Italian comfort food at its finest. But it is also a little heavy for a casual summer dinner. This lightened-up version takes advantage of garden-ripe tomatoes, soft fresh mozzarella, and summery basil. And the best part is that you can do it all outside on the grill.

GRILLED EGGPLANT WITH MOZZARELLA SALAD

Serves 6

1 medium **EGGPLANT**, cut into ½-inch-thick slices

2 large **TOMATOES**, cut into ¼-inch-thick slices

½ pound **FRESH MOZZARELLA** cheese, cut into ¼-inch-thick slices

¼ cup olive oil

Kosher salt and freshly ground black pepper

1 tablespoon extra-virgin olive oil

1 tablespoon balsamic vinegar

½ cup finely sliced **FRESH BASIL** leaves

1 Preheat a grill or grill pan to medium-high heat.

2 Meanwhile, arrange the eggplant, tomatoes, and mozzarella slices on a platter or baking sheet. Drizzle with the olive oil and season with salt and pepper.

3 Put the eggplant on the grill, cover, and cook until nicely grill marked, about 2 minutes. Flip the eggplant, cover, and cook for 2 minutes. Uncover the grill and top each eggplant with a slice of tomato and a few slices of mozzarella. Cover and cook until the mozzarella is melted, about 1 minute.

4 Remove the eggplant from the grill. Drizzle with the extra-virgin olive oil and vinegar, top with the basil, and serve.

I made a dish similar to this on *The Chew* when Hugh Jackman was on the show. He was a great sport, tearing apart the fresh mint like a true Wolverine. This shaved carrot salad has a bit of an Asian flavor profile going on thanks to the scallions, mint, and peanuts. To get the best texture on the carrots, use a mandoline or vegetable peeler to shave off long ribbons.

GRILLED SALMON WITH CARROT & PEANUT SALAD

Serves 4

4 (6-ounce) skinless **SALMON FILLETS**

Kosher salt and freshly ground black pepper

½ cup plus 2 tablespoons extra-virgin olive oil

¼ cup red wine vinegar

1 tablespoon cumin seeds, toasted and ground

3 medium **CARROTS**, shaved (2½ cups)

1 cup thinly sliced **SCALLIONS**, green and white parts

1 cup torn **FRESH MINT** leaves

½ cup **ROASTED PEANUTS**, roughly chopped

1 Preheat a grill or grill pan to medium-high heat.

2 Season the salmon on both sides with salt and pepper. Drizzle with 2 tablespoons of the olive oil and put on the grill. Cover and cook until nicely charred and the fish releases from the grill, about 3 minutes. Flip and cook until medium-rare, about 2 minutes.

3 Meanwhile, in a medium bowl, whisk together the vinegar and remaining ½ cup olive oil. Add the cumin, carrots, scallions, mint, and peanuts, and toss to combine. Taste and adjust the seasoning, adding salt and pepper as needed.

4 Put the salmon on plates, top with the carrot salad, and serve.

2 pounds **FLANK STEAK**

Kosher salt and freshly ground black pepper

4 tablespoons olive oil

½ pound thick-cut **BACON**, diced

4 ears **SWEET CORN**, kernels cut from the cobs (about 3 cups)

Pinch of crushed red pepper flakes

2 tablespoons sherry vinegar

2 cups loosely packed **ARUGULA**

1 small red onion, thinly sliced

In the summer, I am always looking for new ways to use ripe sweet corn (and steak, but that's a year-round obsession). In this recipe, I pair corn-off-the-cob with bacon for a sweet and salty topper for juicy grilled steak. I prefer flank steak cooked no more than medium-rare; remember to let it rest before cutting it against the grain.

GRILLED FLANK STEAK WITH CORN & BACON SALAD

Serves 6

1 Preheat a grill or grill pan to medium-high heat.

2 Season the steak on both sides with salt and black pepper. Drizzle with 3 tablespoons of the olive oil, put on the grill, and cover. Cover and cook until nicely charred and the meat releases from the grill, about 3 minutes. Flip and cook until medium-rare, about 2 minutes.

3 Meanwhile, put a large skillet over medium-high heat. Add the remaining 1 tablespoon olive oil and the bacon and cook until almost crisp, about 2 minutes. Don't drain off the fat. Add the corn and cook for 2 minutes. Add the red pepper flakes and ½ cup water and deglaze the pan, scraping with a wooden spoon to get up the browned bits on the bottom of the pan. Stir in the vinegar. Taste and adjust the seasoning, adding salt and black pepper as needed.

4 Remove the steak to a cutting board and slice against the grain. Top with the corn and bacon, arugula, and onion and serve.

Couscous, a quick-cooking pasta, belongs in every pantry. Like regular pasta, it can be flavored in countless ways. Here, I combine it with tomato, lemon, and mint and use it as a bed for grilled chicken. After steaming, the couscous needs to be fluffed up with a fork to separate the grains and make it light and airy.

GRILLED CHICKEN WITH LEMON COUSCOUS SALAD

Serves 6

Kosher salt and freshly ground black pepper

6 (4-ounce) boneless, skin-on CHICKEN THIGHS, pounded thin

2 tablespoons olive oil

2 (10-ounce) boxes couscous (2 cups)

2 cups halved CHERRY TOMATOES (from 1 pint)

Grated zest and juice of 2 LEMONS

2 GARLIC cloves, minced

½ cup pine nuts, toasted

1 cup chopped FRESH MINT leaves

6 tablespoons extra-virgin olive oil

1 Preheat a grill or grill pan to high heat. Pour 4 cups water into a saucepan, season with salt, cover the pan, and bring to a boil.

2 Season the chicken on both sides with salt and pepper. Drizzle with the olive oil and put skin-side down on the grill. Cover and cook until nicely charred and the meat releases from the grill, about 3 minutes. Flip, cover, and cook until cooked through, about 2 minutes.

3 Meanwhile, in a large heatproof bowl, combine the couscous, tomatoes, lemon zest and juice, and garlic. Add the boiling water, cover tightly with plastic wrap, and set aside until all the liquid has been absorbed, about 4 minutes.

4 Uncover the couscous and add the pine nuts, mint, and extra-virgin olive oil, stirring to fluff the couscous and combine the ingredients. Taste and adjust the seasoning, adding salt and pepper as needed.

5 To serve, spread the couscous onto plates and top with the chicken thighs.

Skirt steak is one of the most affordable yet flavorful cuts of beef on the entire steer. To get the most out of its glory, season it liberally, don't overcook it, let it rest after cooking, and slice it across the grain. I love pairing steak and grilled chicken with this tangy and refreshing chickpea salad. For this recipe—canned chickpeas are fine—just rinse them thoroughly before using.

GRILLED SKIRT STEAK WITH CHICKPEA SALAD

Serves 4

1 pound SKIRT STEAK

1 tablespoon coriander seeds, toasted

Kosher salt and freshly ground black pepper

2 tablespoons olive oil

1 (16-ounce) can chickpeas, rinsed and drained

1 cup thinly sliced SCALLIONS, white and green parts

¼ cup chopped FRESH FLAT-LEAF PARSLEY leaves

2 GARLIC cloves, minced

1 cup GREEK YOGURT

¼ cup extra-virgin olive oil

1 Preheat a grill or grill pan to medium-high heat.

2 Season the steak on both sides with the coriander and salt and pepper. Drizzle with the olive oil and put on the grill. Cover and cook until nicely charred and the meat releases from the grill, about 2 minutes. Flip and cook until medium-rare, about 2 minutes.

3 Meanwhile, in a large bowl, stir together the chickpeas, scallions, parsley, garlic, yogurt, and extra-virgin olive oil. Season with salt and pepper.

4 Thinly slice the skirt steak against the grain. Spread the yogurt onto plates, top with sliced steak, and then cap it off with the chickpea salad. Serve immediately.

2 **GRAPEFRUITS**

1 pound shelled and deveined **LARGE SHRIMP**

Kosher salt and freshly ground black pepper

2 tablespoons olive oil

1 **AVOCADO**, sliced

½ cup sliced **RED ONION**

¼ cup **FRESH FLAT-LEAF PARSLEY** leaves

4 tablespoons extra-virgin olive oil

I know it might sound like needless work to remove all the skin, pith, membranes, and seeds of the grapefruit—a technique chefs call making supremes—but it makes a huge difference in texture and flavor in a citrus salad. Grapefruit pith is especially bitter and inedible. And once you learn, you can use the technique on oranges and other citrus.

GRILLED SHRIMP & GRAPEFRUIT SALAD

Serves 4

1 Use a sharp knife to slice off the tops and bottoms of the grapefruits, removing all of the white pith to expose the fruit. Following the curve of the fruit, slice around the sides to do the same. You should have just juicy grapefruit showing and no white pith or membranes at this point. Use a paring knife to slice between the membranes of each section to remove the segments. Put the segments into a medium bowl, discarding any pits.

2 Preheat a grill or grill pan to medium-high heat.

3 Season the shrimp on both sides with salt and pepper. Drizzle with the olive oil and put on the grill. Grill until cooked through, about 2 minutes per side.

4 Meanwhile, add the avocado, onion, parsley leaves, extra-virgin olive oil, and a good pinch of salt to the grapefruit segments and toss to combine. Taste and adjust the seasoning, adding salt and pepper as needed.

5 Put the shrimp on plates, top with the grapefruit salad, and serve.

Of all the ways that I've prepared and eaten zucchini, the best recipes always involve raw—not cooked—zucchini. In summer, when these veggies are everywhere, I love preparing simple salads like this one that take advantage of the season. Look for small, tender zukes, because the older ones tend to get bitter.

GRILLED SALMON & SHAVED ZUCCHINI SALAD

Serves 4

4 (6-ounce) skinless **SALMON FILLETS**

Kosher salt and freshly ground black pepper

2 tablespoons olive oil

Grated zest and juice of 2 **LEMONS**

1 **GARLIC** clove, minced

¼ cup chopped **FRESH DILL**

6 tablespoons extra-virgin olive oil

2 small **ZUCCHINI**, thinly sliced into rounds (about 3 cups)

1 Preheat a grill or grill pan to medium-high heat.

2 Season the salmon on both sides with salt and pepper. Drizzle with the olive oil and put on the grill. Cover and cook until nicely charred and the fish releases from the grill, about 3 minutes. Flip and cook until medium-rare, about 2 minutes.

3 Meanwhile, in a medium bowl, whisk together the lemon zest and juice, garlic, dill, and extra-virgin olive oil. Add the zucchini and toss to combine. Taste and adjust the seasoning, adding salt and pepper as needed.

4 Put the salmon on plates, top with the zucchini salad, and serve.

In Latin America, grilled meats are often served with *chimichurri*, a bright-green salsa made with heaps of parsley, garlic, and vinegar, much like this sauce. The tart and tangy sauce is the perfect accompaniment to richly flavored beef. Season the meat liberally, don't overcook it, let it rest after cooking, and slice it against the grain.

GRILLED SKIRT STEAK WITH PARSLEY SAUCE

Serves 4

1 pound SKIRT STEAK

Kosher salt and freshly ground black pepper

2 tablespoons olive oil

2½ teaspoons sherry vinegar

2 GARLIC cloves, roughly chopped

2 cups FRESH FLAT-LEAF PARSLEY leaves

1 JALAPEÑO, seeds and ribs removed, roughly chopped

½ cup SLICED ALMONDS

¾ cup extra-virgin olive oil

1 Preheat a grill or grill pan to medium-high heat.

2 Season the steak on both sides with salt and pepper. Drizzle with the olive oil and put on the grill. Cover and cook until nicely charred and the meat releases from the grill, about 2 minutes. Flip and cook until medium-rare, about 2 minutes.

3 Meanwhile, in a blender or food processor, combine the vinegar, garlic, parsley, jalapeño, almonds, ½ teaspoon salt, and the extra-virgin olive oil. Blend or puree until smooth.

4 Thinly slice the skirt steak against the grain. Put the steak on plates, top with the parsley sauce, and serve.

I can't think of too many foods that are more refreshing than a cucumber and dill salad. And since dill works so well with salmon, I thought, *why not put the two together?* The beauty of this dish is that even though it's a natural for summer, it can be enjoyed all year long.

GRILLED SALMON WITH SHAVED CUCUMBERS

Serves 4

4 (6-ounce) skinless **SALMON FILLETS**

Kosher salt and freshly ground black pepper

1 teaspoon fennel seeds

2 tablespoons olive oil

1 tablespoon white wine vinegar

½ cup **SOUR CREAM**

3 tablespoons roughly chopped **FRESH DILL**

1 **ENGLISH CUCUMBER**, cut into ⅛-inch-thick slices

⅓ cup thinly sliced **RED ONION**

1 Preheat a grill or grill pan to medium-high heat.

2 Season the salmon on both sides with salt, pepper, and the fennel seeds, patting them in to help them stick. Drizzle with the olive oil and put on the grill. Cover and cook until nicely charred and the fish releases from the grill, about 3 minutes. Flip and cook until medium-rare, about 2 minutes.

3 Meanwhile, in a medium bowl, whisk together the vinegar, sour cream, and dill. Add the cucumber and red onion and toss to combine. Season with salt and pepper.

4 Put the salmon on plates, top with the cucumber salad, and serve.

Prosciutto-wrapped figs are an Italian delight, the sweet summer-ripe fruit concealed beneath the salty, porky ham. This dish plays off that great pork-and-fig pairing, but with meaty ham steaks instead of the pricy prosciutto. Be careful when grilling the ham because the honey in the glaze can go from nicely charred to burnt in no time flat.

GRILLED HAM STEAK WITH FIGS & ARUGULA

Serves 4

2 tablespoons honey

1 tablespoon Dijon mustard

¼ cup balsamic vinegar

½ cup extra-virgin olive oil

1 tablespoon chopped **FRESH ROSEMARY** leaves

Kosher salt and freshly ground black pepper

4 (7-ounce) **HAM STEAKS**, each ½ inch thick

3 cups loosely packed **ARUGULA**

8 **FRESH FIGS**, quartered

1 Preheat a grill or grill pan to high heat.

2 In a medium bowl, whisk together the honey, mustard, vinegar, olive oil, rosemary, and a good bit of pepper. Pour half of the vinaigrette into a small bowl to brush on the ham steaks. Reserve the remaining vinaigrette in the bowl to toss with the arugula and figs later.

3 Brush both sides of the ham steaks with vinaigrette and put them on the grill. Cover and cook until nicely charred, about 2 minutes. Flip, brush with more of the vinaigrette, and cook until nicely charred, about 2 minutes.

4 Add the arugula and figs to the bowl with the reserved vinaigrette. Toss to combine and season with salt and pepper.

5 Put the ham steaks on plates, top with the fig and arugula salad, and serve.

GRILLED PEACHES & HONEY SUNDAE 212

WHISKEY CARAMEL SUNDAE 213

WARM CHOCOLATE & CHILE SUNDAE 216

TART CHERRY & RED WINE SUNDAE 217

CARAMELIZED BANANA SUNDAE 218

SALTED CARAMEL SUNDAE WITH PEANUTS 219

I SCREAM, YOU SCREAM SCREAM

PERSONALLY, I don't have much of a sweet tooth. I'd rather just finish a meal with some fresh fruit. But I do have a weakness for ice cream. I can take down a pint of the good stuff like nobody's business.

While there are lots of fancy ice creams with creative flavors on the market these days, I typically prefer just to buy some good old vanilla bean and jazz it up myself. I don't profess to be a pastry chef, but I do know how to whip up a tasty ice cream sauce! And once you add sauce to ice cream—and maybe a little fruit—all of a sudden you have a sundae. That is my secret to last-minute desserts.

In summer, when peaches are in season and the grill is already glowing, it's so easy to toss some fruit on the barbie after you pull off the meat. Grilling fruit intensifies the sweetness, so when you start with ripe, juicy, sweet-as-sugar peaches, you end up with something out of this world. The lemon juice keeps things in balance.

GRILLED PEACHES & HONEY SUNDAE

Serves 4

2 **PEACHES**, halved

1 tablespoon **UNSALTED BUTTER**, melted

Juice of ½ **LEMON**

3 tablespoons honey

1 pint **VANILLA BEAN ICE CREAM**

1 Preheat a grill or grill pan to medium-high heat.

2 Brush the peaches on both sides with the melted butter, then put cut-side down on the grill. Cook until slightly charred, about 2 minutes per side.

3 Remove the peaches from the grill and cut in half to create 8 quarters. In a medium bowl, toss the warm peaches, lemon juice, and honey.

4 Spoon a large scoop of vanilla ice cream into each of 4 bowls, top with 2 peach quarters and some of their juices, and serve.

This is one for the adults in the crowd. While whiskey is good enough to drink straight, of course, cooking with it adds pleasant notes of oak and butterscotch, which go great with caramel sauce. Don't cook with any booze that you wouldn't drink!

WHISKEY CARAMEL SUNDAE

Serves 4

1 cup **HEAVY CREAM**

2 tablespoons **WHISKEY**

1 cup sugar

2 tablespoons **UNSALTED BUTTER**

Pinch of kosher salt

1 pint **VANILLA BEAN ICE CREAM**

1 In a small saucepan, combine the cream and whiskey and bring to a simmer over low heat.

2 In a medium saucepan, combine the sugar and 3 tablespoons water. With a wet pastry brush, wipe down the insides of the pan to make sure there are no sugar crystals sticking to the side. Put the pan over high heat, cover (which helps prevent crystallization), and bring to a boil. Cook for 3 minutes without stirring. Uncover and check the color. If the boiling sugar mixture is still pale, cover the pan and continue cooking until light amber, about 1 minute. Uncover and swirl the pan to gently mix the sugar mixture.

3 When the sugar becomes golden brown, remove it from the heat and slowly whisk in the warm cream mixture. Return to low heat and add the butter and salt, whisking until the butter is melted and fully incorporated. The sauce is ready to be served but will continue to thicken as it sits. If the sauce gets too thick, reheat over low heat to loosen it.

4 Spoon a large scoop of vanilla ice cream into each of 4 bowls, top with whiskey caramel sauce, and serve.

Chocolate sauce is so easy to make that I don't understand why people ever buy it. Seriously, it doesn't take very long and, because you buy the ingredients, you can be sure that they are good quality (which is not something I can say about all the bottled stuff). Adding just a hint of spice to the warm sauce makes the chilly ice cream all the more refreshing!

WARM CHOCOLATE & CHILE SUNDAE

Serves 4

1 cup **HEAVY CREAM**

1 cinnamon stick

¼ teaspoon ancho chile powder

¼ teaspoon cayenne pepper

¼ cup sugar

Pinch of kosher salt

4 ounces **SEMISWEET CHOCOLATE**, chopped

1 tablespoon **UNSWEETENED COCOA POWDER**

1 pint **VANILLA BEAN ICE CREAM**

1 Put a medium saucepan over medium heat. Add the cream, cinnamon stick, chile powder, cayenne, sugar, and salt and cook until the sugar dissolves and the mixture reaches a simmer, about 4 minutes.

2 Remove the cinnamon stick, add the chopped chocolate and cocoa powder, and whisk constantly until the chocolate is melted. Bring the mixture to a gentle boil and then remove from the heat.

3 Spoon a large scoop of vanilla ice cream into each of 4 bowls, top with chocolate sauce, and serve.

This sauce is a lot like those wonderful mulled wine drinks, which are made with fruit and spices and served warm. Simmering cherries in wine flavors both the fruit and the booze—a win-win! For this, I'd use a rich red with mellow oakiness, like a merlot. The vinegar at the end makes sure this combo doesn't end up syrupy-sweet and one-note.

TART CHERRY & RED WINE SUNDAE

Serves 4

2 cups **FROZEN CHERRIES**

1 cinnamon stick

½ cup sugar

1 tablespoon cornstarch

1 cup dry **RED WINE**

1 teaspoon red wine vinegar

1 pint **VANILLA BEAN ICE CREAM**

1 Put a large saucepan over medium-high heat. Add the cherries, cinnamon stick, sugar, and cornstarch and cook until the sugar starts to melt, about 1 minute. Add the wine, bring the mixture to a boil, and cook until the wine has reduced and is slightly thickened, about 4 minutes.

2 Remove from the heat, remove the cinnamon stick, and stir in the vinegar.

3 Spoon a large scoop of vanilla ice cream into each of 4 bowls, top with warm cherries and red wine sauce, and serve.

If you've ever tried Bananas Foster, then you know how good caramelized bananas are on ice cream. This is a quick version of that classic dessert, but we skip the flaming booze part, which can be hazardous to eyebrows! I like the addition of orange juice, which adds some of the fruitiness lost by omitting the rum.

CARAMELIZED BANANA SUNDAE

Serves 4

½ cup packed dark brown sugar

¼ teaspoon ground cinnamon

Pinch of kosher salt

2 tablespoons UNSALTED BUTTER

2 BANANAS, halved lengthwise and then crosswise

¼ cup fresh-squeezed orange juice

1 pint VANILLA BEAN ICE CREAM

1 In a small bowl, combine the brown sugar, cinnamon, and salt.

2 Put a large skillet over medium heat.

3 Add the butter to the preheated skillet and then add the bananas, cut-side down. Cook until they begin to caramelize, about 1 minute. Flip and then reduce the heat to medium-low. Sprinkle the brown sugar mixture over the bananas. Pour in the orange juice and cook, swirling the pan to melt the sugar and coat the bananas, for 1 minute. Turn off the heat.

4 Spoon a large scoop of vanilla ice cream into each of 4 bowls, top with warm bananas and caramel sauce, and serve.

Sweet and salty is the greatest flavor combination there is. Think about chocolate-covered pretzels, sugared pecans, or even watermelon and feta salad—yum! The roasted nuts in this dessert add another salty, crunchy dimension to an already addictive combination.

SALTED CARAMEL SUNDAE WITH PEANUTS

Serves 4

1 cup **HEAVY CREAM**

1 cup **SUGAR**

2 tablespoons **UNSALTED BUTTER**

½ teaspoon salt

1 pint **VANILLA BEAN ICE CREAM**

1 cup **ROASTED PEANUTS**

1 In a small saucepan, bring the cream to a simmer over low heat.

2 In a medium saucepan, combine the sugar and 3 tablespoons water. With a wet pastry brush, wipe down the insides of the pan to make sure there are no sugar crystals sticking to the side. Put the pan over high heat, cover (which helps prevent crystallization), and bring to a boil. Cook for 3 minutes without stirring. Uncover and check the color. If the boiling sugar mixture is still pale, cover and continue cooking until light amber, about 1 minute. Uncover and swirl the pan to gently mix the sugar mixture.

3 When the sugar becomes golden brown, remove it from the heat and slowly whisk in the warm cream. Return to low heat and add the butter and salt, whisking until the butter is melted and fully incorporated. The sauce is ready to be served but will continue to thicken as it sits. If the sauce gets too thick, reheat over low heat to loosen it.

4 Spoon a large scoop of vanilla ice cream into each of 4 bowls, top with warm caramel sauce and peanuts, and serve.

ACKNOWLEDGMENTS

Although my name is on the cover of this cookbook, it wouldn't be if it weren't for an entire team of supportive people.

First of all, I'd like to thank my culinary assistant, **Katie Pickens**, whose exhaustive recipe testing ensures that all of the dishes featured in this book will come out just as good when you cook them at home.

Thanks, too, go out to **Douglas Trattner**, who helps me organize my words, thoughts, and concepts so that they materialize on the page even better than I envisioned them.

This cookbook would not look as beautiful as it does without the stunning food photography of **Jennifer May**, who also happens to be an absolute joy to work with.

Without my amazing assistant, **Rebecca Yody**, my life would very likely grind to a halt. She really does keep my life in order (and my sanity in place).

My heartfelt appreciation also goes out to my business partner, **Doug Petkovic**, who works around the clock to make sure that all of our restaurants run like a top. My main man in the kitchen, **Derek "Powder" Clayton**, works just as hard to maintain our incredibly high culinary standards. Hats off to the entire team at **Two Twelve Management**, **Becca Parrish and the pros at Becca PR**, and everybody at the **Food Network**. Special thanks to *The Chew* **crew** and **ABC** for letting me do "5 in 5," and for allowing me to have so much fun every day at work.

And because she puts up with my inexhaustible procrastination efforts, I must thank my editor, **Rica Allannic**. Without her this book would still be in my head rather than in your hands where it belongs.

Thank you!

INDEX

Note: Page references in *italics* indicate photographs.